PRAYER IS WARFARE

formerly
Prayer, God's Power Through Man

PRAYER IS WARFARE

Formerly
PRAYER,
GOD'S POWER
THROUGH MAN

By
Mickey Bonner

MICKEY BONNER EVANGELISTIC ASSOCIATION
P.O. BOX 90593
HOUSTON, TEXAS 77290

ISBN 1-878578-00-6

Published by Mickey Bonner Evangelistic Association
P.O. Box 90593, Houston, Texas 77290
Printed in the United States of America

DEDICATION

To my son Mickey, one who was born on my birthday and has since been a delight to my life. My greatest desire for him is that he become a man of answered prayer.

Mickey Bonner

CONTENTS

FOREWORD

When I was asked to write the foreword for this book, my first thoughts were, "Surely there is no need for another book on 'prayer.' " All of my ministry I have tried to keep up with all the material on prayer. After going over the manuscript of this new book, it was thrilling to grasp some fresh nuggets from God's gold mine of truth. Again, I marveled at the Word of God as never being exhausted and the men God uses to open truth to us. Among those men is the author of this book, Mickey Bonner.

Anyone who has ever heard Mickey Bonner preach will be delighted to know of the new book on prayer. He has been used of God to enlighten the saints of God concerning their throne rights and privileges. Those who know his ministry will not be disappointed with this book. It reflects Mr. Bonner's ability to unfold treasures of truth from the scriptures, combined with the rare gift of making it apply to life as we all know it.

In order to make this book interesting, we must not be satisfied to get a prayer through occasionally. There must be a desire for a more satisfying prayer life, one that elevates and purifies every act of the body and mind and integrates the entire personality into a single spiritual unit. Seeking to walk with God is shown to be a life of constant communion where all thoughts and acts are prayers and the entire life becomes one holy sacrifice of praise and worship.

Here is a work from one of God's choice servants that is a must for every believer. There is a refreshing wealth of information which comes from a hunger and thirst after God.

The whole book is easy to read and yet confronts us to practice what we read. This book merits a wide circulation and we trust will be a source of inspiration to thousands of Christians who may or may not have had the privilege of sitting under Mickey Bonner's ministry.

Evangelist Bill Stafford

INTRODUCTION

The object of this book is to bring to light one of the most important principles of prayer and that is the conducting of warfare against Satan. To not understand this is to miss totally what God is wanting to do through the life of an individual Christian. In this volume we will take Scriptural positions promised to the Christian and share, first of all, their conditions to the Christian and then their power through that committed individual.

By conditions, I mean that God places with answered prayer a price that must first be paid by the believer—that is, a walk with Christ in such a deep way that he is by intuitive revelation able to hear from God. This principle we will share in a later chapter; however, it involves being able to discern what is "bound or loosed" in Heaven and acting upon it in faith.

Throughout this entire writing you will find one principle woven through the fabric of its purpose, and that is, that "prayer is finding the mind of God and agreeing with it in faith."

To enter into the battle against Satan, you must realize that it is God's power that defeats the devil. In order to engage that Heavenly force, God is seeking an intercessor that will stand against the wiles of the devil and allow God to defeat his stronghold in a life or a circumstance. Prayer is the greatest force known to man. Its Biblical experiences include the parting of the sea, the flowing of water from a rock, the stopping of the sun, the shutting off of rain, the calling of fire from Heaven. Other experiences include Jesus' feeding of 5,000, his making the blind to see, the lame to walk, the deaf to hear, and the sparing of all mankind, when He who knew no sin became sin for the world and cried in prayer, "Father, forgive them for they know not what they do."

Prayer, its power, is taught in the Word; its purpose is to pursue the will of God; its plan is for man's obedience to God's will. The ultimate experience by the Christian is "Prayer, God's Power Through Man."

Here is the path to its manifestation through the life of the Christian.

CHAPTER ONE

WHY PRAYER IS NOT ANSWERED

In this chapter we will deal with the life of the Christian. How many times have I heard someone testify, "As far as I know I have never had one prayer answered"? There are two reasons for this. First, this person could be lost. This is best explained in John 9:31 (KJV):

"Now we know that God heareth not sinners: but if any man be a worshipper of God, and doeth his will, him he heareth."

In this verse we find the formula for both positions —*lost* or *born again.*

First He says that we know that God heareth not sinners. In a further chapter we will discuss the hearing from Heaven as Christ heard in order that we might agree with what is heard. Herein lies the position of answered prayer—that which is *bound and loosed.*

GARAGE RELIGION

However, the point here is that God does not hear the petitions of a lost man. In fact, the only prayer

1

He hears from an unsaved person is one that is coming from a broken, contrite heart, sickened by its own sin, crying out to God, "Save me, I'm lost." From that posture, God will then reach down from Heaven and save that individual. The Bible teaches, "No man cometh to the Father except the Spirit draw him." Therefore, it is not being born in a Christian family, or a Christian nation, that makes a man a Christian. It is only when he sees himself as God sees him that he cries out to be saved. God says, "Ye must be born again." He also says, "It is not of yourselves, it is the gift of God."

Someone has well said that being born in a Christian family will no more make you a born again child of God than being born in a garage will make you a car. However, we are living today in the midst of this kind of religion. The vast majority of all those professing Christ have never possessed Him. They have been physically born into a Christian family, or joined by catechism, or baptism, or whatever. However, for the most part they have met a plan, but have never met the Man, Christ Jesus. What a tragedy! To someday go out of this life having been religious but lost—dying in their sins.

A good test to your salvation experience is, have you ever had a specific answer to a prayer? One that you could nail down as God-planned, and which you prayed in agreement with Him—something so supernatural that the only explanation for the circumstance from beginning to end was God? If not, then before you can move to answered prayer, there is a need to go back to the cross and settle the issue of your own heart. Again, to be saved means to have one's self so open to God that you come under conviction due to the sin in your life. In fact, you grieve so over your lost condition that in your desperation you cry out to God, "Forgive me of my sins—I declare them all under the Blood of Jesus Christ—every sin I have ever committed I bring to the cross, and now, Lord Jesus, please come into my heart—I must have you—I cannot go another moment without you— save me! Thank you for saving me! I praise your wonderful name for my everlasting life! I thank you! I am born again!"

Do you know what? If you are broken by God's revealing Himself to you that you might see yourself as you really are, and you have cried out for salvation, you were saved. As a saved person, you are ready to move into the most powerful position known to man —that is, answered prayer. You might say, "Out of the garage and into the garden."

RECKLESS DRIVER

Now let's look again to John 9:31. God says that He does not hear sinners. As we shared with you earlier, this includes two positions: 1) the lost who have no answered prayers, and 2) the saved who are out of the will of God. It is to the latter we refer now.

There are many verses that emphatically deal with this subject; however, we will speak only of those most relevant to this writing.

In Matthew 6:14-15 (AMP) we find:

"For if you forgive people their trespasses—that is, their reckless and wilful sins, leaving them, letting them go and giving up resentment— your heavenly Father will also forgive you.

But if you do not forgive others their trespasses—their reckless and wilful sins, leaving them, letting them go and giving up resentment—neither will your Father forgive you your trespasses."

In a later chapter we are going to deal with the real meaning of the Lord's Prayer. However, let's look at the two verses that immediately follow Christ's specific rule on coming into the Father's presence.

His first statement in verse fourteen is, "For if you forgive people their trespasses—that is their reckless and willful sins . . ." Please notice the use of *if* before the clarification of the position the Christian must take. That is unless we do these things demanded by God our prayer will not be answered. What are these things.?

First, forgive reckless sins—a reckless sin is one that was done against a person without premeditation. An example of this would be someone who was drunk or high on drugs driving a car at a high rate of speed, losing control of his vehicle, crashing into someone he loves, taking his life or health. Another circumstance that we so often hear of is someone playing with a so-called unloaded pistol and accidentally taking another's life. In the process, bitterness is rooted deep in the heart of an individual. If this is so in the life of the Christian, then as we will see scripturally, he has no answered prayer. The prerequisite to all prayer is forgiveness as well as confession of sins.

You must stand forgiving to be forgiven. We have just completed a book, *God Can Heal Your Mind*, dealing with unforgiveness as a root of bitterness. How many times in counseling have we found those who have missed God's perfect plan for their lives

(Ephesians 2:10) by not being able to praise God for all things! It must be done so that Satan can be neutralized from strongholds of the past. If Christ had held anything in His heart against His oppressors, we could not be *saved by grace through faith*. He would have failed in living the sinless life. Our propitiation could not be real. The fact that Christ was without sin gives us the door through which we may volitionally walk, having our sins covered by His blood. Not to forgive those who have recklessly sinned against us is, again, to deny Christ His *reasonable* control of our lives (Rom. 12:1-2). Be assured if there is unforgiveness, there can be no answered prayer. Don't you be as reckless in your spiritual life as the driver in the illustration—to go about in your life separated from God's flow through you is to do it with recklessness. How tragic! No answered prayer!

SHOOT OUT

Looking further in this verse, Christ then uses the term, wilful. Now this means to be done with intent —planned and purposed for the harm or destruction of another's life or possessions. This is perhaps the hardest situation of all to overcome—to praise God for. However, it must be done in order to be set in a position to have answered prayer. Before this chapter is completed, there is a verse that will be explained as to why prayer cannot be answered with bitterness in the heart. Again, you must forgive to be forgiven.

A favorite tool of Satan's is to get a Christian who is making an effort to *run the race* to look over his shoulder at past things. In counselling, we have found that the greatest deterrent to being *free indeed* is unforgiveness toward self or others. If the devil can get you to look back on your life, he can cause you to stumble and fall in your Christian walk. Then comes the effort to restart, as so many times in the past. Basketball Christianity (high one minute and low the next) is always played by Satan's rules. His game plan is to, by *wiles,* destroy any effort you make toward going on with God. I am reminded of a situation that occurred several years ago. A pastor's wife called and asked if I would counsel by telephone a member of their church. Her problem was that every time she began a deeper walk with Christ, something would happen and she would lose the position gained. She was distraught because she had a deep desire to go on with God. After consenting to minister to that individual, I discovered the person in need was on an extension phone listening. After our introduction, I was immediately impressed that she had deep bitterness in her life. I asked her what had happened that caused this in her heart. From the first moment of our conversation there was a softness in her voice; however, she instantly changed at my question. She began to tell me of an incident which had happened in her life in the last several months. In fact, it was through this incident she had been brought to Christ.

The event was that her mother had been shot and killed by the man she was dating. I did not ask for further details, but I had gathered from the conversation that there was insane jealousy involved on his part. As she shared this tragedy, she stated that her mother had been taken away from her. As the conversation continued, her voice became more harsh. I finally asked her what she would do if she met this man on the street.

She said, "I would shoot him. I would kill him if I could." At this point she was crying.

I then asked her how much she loved the Lord Jesus. In a change of voice she said, "With all my heart."

I asked her what it meant to her to serve Him. Her reply was, "Everything."

I then read her these verses and finished by saying that she would never know the fullness of the person of Christ, in her life, until she could put her bitterness under the Blood. (It must be understood that we are forgiven at the level that we forgive [Matthew 6:14-15].) She then would need to seek God's daily help in forgiving those who had taken her mother's life. (The question is often asked, "How long are we to continue to deal with the act of forgiveness?" The answer is, until the bondage is broken and Satan can no longer accuse you with the circumstance. It is probably best explained, until you can talk about it openly without becoming emotional.)

She instantly became angry and said, "I cannot do that. I will not do that."

As we continued with several verses on forgiveness as a prerequisite to Christ's control, she became even more adamant regarding the circumstance.

Knowing that she must be shocked into facing the issue Biblically, I then stated, "Please do not bother me with this until you are ready to come to terms with God's position in the matter."

As I made sounds of closing the conversation and hanging up, she said, "Please wait."

I then asked her what was most important — her feelings or God's will.

After a moment of silence she stated, "God's will."

I said, "All right, I want you, right now, to praise God for His bringing to your life forgiveness."

She again hesitated, but finally said, "Lord, I praise You, that in You, I can forgive the one who took my mother's life."

I asked her to say it again. She did; only this time she broke in her will. As she began to cry, I then asked her to pray for this man as she forgave him. Upon doing that, Christ took the load from her life. During this wonderful event she began sobbing and praising the Lord at the same time. FREE!

It was time to ask the most important question, and that was, "If you met this man on the street, what would you do?"

Her reply was, "I would tell him about Jesus Christ, and what he has done for me." She was free.

Herein lies the quality of these two verses, for God is emphatic when He says that we are to leave these things. We are to *let them go.* We are to give up resentment. Have you done this? Are all the things in your past life forgiven and forgotten? Are you *pressing on to the prize?* Or are you still holding on to unforgiveness that, like a *root of bitterness,* keeps springing up to trip you up in your going on with Christ. You see, you must forgive in order for your Heavenly Father to forgive you. It must be done. For you not to forgive is to be unforgiven by God. And to be unforgiven by God means no position of prayer, separated, without power, without joy, or peace, or victory, unfulfilled, fruitless, and bound by Satan. Again, how tragic!

You see, there are many verses that amplify this position of separation from God's power. In Psalms 66:18, we find: "If I regard iniquity in my heart, the Lord will not hear me."

What is iniquity? It is to knowingly have a sin in

your life that you will not deal with. To regard means, for the most part, to cohabitate—as in this case, to try to live with the circumstance. If you know you have sin in your life and you are not willing to deal with it, you have regarded iniquity in your person. God says this separates you from being heard by Him in your prayers. *God will not hear me*, is the declared position of this verse.

What is in your life that causes this situation—unforgiveness, or perhaps the unwillingness to let go of an area of your life that you know to be sin? Is this separation from God's power worth it?

The greatest praying is done in a crisis. When one comes face to face with a deep problem, it is at that point one gets serious. It is well said that prayer is not the position of the body but the condition of the heart. Again, what is your sin? Is it worth being separated from God? Why not break the power of cancelled sin in your life and let Christ control you? You will never be happier. You say, "It's too much to forgive or overcome." Let me again share another verse regarding this position.

In Isaiah 59:2, God says,

"But your iniquities have separated between you and your God, and your sins have hid his face from you, that he will not hear." (KJV)

Here we find again that iniquity has separated you and your God. Iniquities are those things hidden and harbored in unconfession or unforgiveness—those deep things that hold more regard in your personality than do God's plan and purpose for your life. Again, God states emphatically in His Word that this person has no power with God. There is an old saying that if you want something done, find someone that is busy and ask him to do it. The outward sign of his business shows that he will get it done. By the same token, if you want some word from God through prayer, find someone who is used to having answered prayer and who is busy praying to stand with you touching your circumstance. The secret is brokenness —broken over the sins of your own life. Confess the guilt, claim God's promise of I John 1:9. Then as you pray, *stand forgiving*. How precious is the promise of answered prayer! How beautiful is the knowledge that God has used you in an eternal situation by your obedience to His Will!

However, if you are not willing to be broken to be used, the rest of Isaiah 59:2 describes your position entirely, for God says, "And your sins have hidden His face from you that He will not hear."

And that *tells the tale.* Your known sin has hidden His face from you. As we will study later, this means He will not reveal His Will and plan in a matter to you. God answers no prayers but His own, and to be unable to hear from Heaven and to agree makes the Christian powerless and, for the most part, useless in the Kingdom of God. Some have said, "When I pray I just can't seem to get through." Well, it's not our getting through to God; it is our being in such a position to allow Him to get through to us. His hidden face is due to the sins in our lives. We must be confessed up. Or to coin a phrase I once heard preached by a marvelous preacher, we must be *fessed up daily* to walk in the Kingdom of God and to know His wonderful plan for our lives.

I know this has been shared several times in this volume, but it must be said again, for repetition is the greatest form of learning.

To have answered prayer, these following events must take place in the life:

1) The lost person must be convicted of his sin and through real repentance cry out for Christ to save him. He must be born again.

2) The saved person must confess his sins, and in that state of repentance forgive those who have spitefully used him and persecuted him. He must forgive to be forgiven. He must have settled all past circumstances of sin in his life, and if restitution is called for, it must be done.

It must be done. The things mentioned above will place you into position to be able to hear from God, to enter into the battle and win every time. (The battle is the Lord's.)

So much more is given to us in the Bible regarding these conditions expressed by God, and it is suggested here that you study these carefully. Also, many sins could be named even as those listed in Gal. 5:19-21; however, in this volume we shall deal now with answered prayer—a subject so few are familiar with. The door to enter into this posture is to be *fessed up and right with God.*

CHAPTER TWO

PRAYER IS WARFARE

One of the most important things to be understood about prayer is that it is actually taking ground away from Satan. It is the means by which to move into circumstances or situations and release the bondage in the lives of the individuals involved. Understanding this principle places the person praying into a new dimension. Rote praying, such as quoted prayers, have no power whatsoever in the influence of the Spirit of God over Satan's dominion. To understand God's flow through the individual into the matters at hand is to know that Satan can be defeated only by God. And he was defeated at the cross by the blood of Jesus Christ. The work of Calvary which included death, burial and resurrection, was that which wrote, ''Finish,'' across any powers that Satan might have. Because of this, the Bible is filled with promises on the basis of destroying Satan's hold and bondage. Our position with the devil is to be in an aggressive posture. We are to run fearlessly toward his strongholds and bring them down. Our authority to do this is in the person of Christ Who lives within the Christian. We have the privileged right of coming against those gates that Satan has placed. In Christ's dealing with His disciples in Matthew 16, He asked the question about who men say that He is.

CHIP OFF THE OLD BLOCK

Their answer was, "Some say John the Baptist, others say Elijah and others Jeremiah or one of the prophets."

However, Christ, in emphasizing the position of these men, asked, "Who do you say that I am?"

And Simon Peter made the statement, "Thou art the Christ, the Son of the living God."

Now upon hearing that, Jesus made the statement to Peter, "Blessed art thou Simon Barjonah, for flesh and blood have not revealed it unto thee, but my Father who is in Heaven." And then He went on to share with Peter, who at the moment of his declaration was filled with the Spirit, for his statement was by pure revelation from God. Christ's statement to him was, ". . . Thou art Peter and upon this rock I will build my church and the gates of hell shall not prevail against it."

Now before you go in a direction of misunderstanding about this man's personal position as being the head of the beginning church history, I must share that what Christ was saying to Peter was that He would build His church not upon Peter, but upon Himself. In fact, in His statement to Peter, He used a word that means a piece of stone. The word was *petros*. But when He used the word I, He said *petra*, which means a huge, massive stone or rock such as the Rock of Gibraltar. And so, in essence, what He was saying to Peter was that he was just a *chip off the old block*. Now every child of God, born again, Spirit indwelt, is also that same chip off the old block. And when the true ministry of prayer comes through the life of that individual, he then, by God's power, is aggressively demanding Satan's bondage to be broken in the matter for which he is praying. All Christians have the right to challenge Satan and to bring down his forces in themselves as well as those around them. This is done through warfare praying. The average Christian is not aware of what prayer really is. To some, it is the position of the body; however, it is not the position of the body; it is the condition of the heart. History has shown that some of the greatest prayer warriors lay prostrate in illness or age in their bodies. Some were incapacitated, unable to move or to have a full, meaningful, flowing physical life, and yet in their relationship of righteousness (right standing with God), they were able to be consumed with God's plan. In the lives of prayer warriors like these is a marvelous, powerful, Satan-binding position of prayer that is usable by God in these end-time days. All real prayer is warfare.

PRAISE IS A SWORD

Now there are two kinds of praying in this sense. One is prayer which means to remove the bondage and the other is praise, which brings glory to God. Praise also is a form of warfare and, if understood, can be used very definitely that way. Psalms 149:6 says, "Let the high praises of God be in their mouth and a two edged sword in their hand." In this case praise is used as an offensive weapon to bring down Satan's power. Again, understand that prayer is not a *defensive* posture. It is *offensive* posture. If the Christian is committed, walking in Jesus and filled with His Spirit according to the Word of God, his life is taken care of. His needs are met before he asks. However, he must daily confess his sins so that restitution and spiritual restoration may come. This is mandatory to the Christian who is filled with the Spirit and walking with Jesus Christ (Ephesians 5:16). A sign of prayerful maturity is that one does not form his prayers inwardly, other than standing against sin in his own heart by confession, but outwardly, by receiving God's revelation that through prayer he may bring release, victory or intercession in a circumstance (Proverbs 16:3).

Praise again is a form of prayer and we can use praise against Satanic dominion or oppression. In doing so, Satan will always pull back. Again the verse says praise is a two edged sword. It becomes so only when it reaches *high praise*. Now the difference between praise and high praise is that when man praises God in his flesh, that is praise without power. However, when God takes it away from man and begins to praise Himself through the individual's spirit, then it takes a higher plane of worship or warfare.

An illustration of this is to be in a song service where the music of adoration to God becomes so moving that it is no longer singing, but becomes God glorifying Himself. At the beginning there is praise, but because of your fellowship in the Spirit, you move into high praise. It is that kind of praise or praying that defeats Satan and strips him of power. Again, the Christian must not be in a defensive posture, but is to act in aggression against known strongholds. The Christian must realize that the devil can do no more than God allows. He was defeated at the cross as well as being cast out of Heaven (Ezekiel 28).

Therefore, we have the right to bring Satan to his knees and render him powerless. We are not to be defensive; we are to be offensive.

DEALING WITH THE DEVIL

I once had a pastor who shared with me that he had made a deal with the devil—if Satan would leave him alone, he would leave him alone. Tragically, this man meant it, and as I was sharing with him spiritual warfare, he did not want to hear it. Now this is not negative confession, but you can know the level of a Christian's walk by his fruits. It is evident that this man's ministry had absolutely failed. There was evidence of no power or glory in his life. His only hope was man-designed programs to keep his people physically involved enough to be pacified in their carnal state.

Praise is a power in the hands of the Christian to move against demonic influence, for God establishes this in Psalms 149:7. Here He states that the praise that is high praise from God flowing through the individual will ". . . Execute vengeance upon the nations and punishments upon the people." Then He declares that praise will

> *"Bind their kings with chains and their nobles with fetters of iron. To execute upon them the judgement written, this honor hath all His Saints, Praise Ye the Lord."*

Now is this a physical battle which the Christian enters? No, it is not. When you understand the principles of Ephesians 6, that Satan has his kingdom set up in *principalities and powers*, you will then know that praise literally goes in and disarms and breaks the strongholds. It destroys the demons' binding whether there be one or a legion. Praise is a form of prayer. It is God's power (through the Christian) overcoming the devil to disarm and disrupt him in the area of strongholds. It is amazing that Christians are blinded to this power. When we are aware of atmospheric hindrances in our worship services, hindering the flow of the Holy Spirit, we just simply stop where we are. We then have the people quote aloud, John 3:16. During this time we actually become aware of the oppression lifting and the air clearing. Another way to use the weapon of praise effectively is in situations of stress or conflict, to begin to praise the Lord. This can be done by outwardly confessing and praising Him or inwardly sharing with Him how much you love Him. I find that in moments of problems or stress in my own heart, that in the midst of the battle in which Satan has placed me, I begin to share with Christ that I love Him. I thank Him and praise Him for my salvation and for the joy of life and the victory of heart. It is then that I find a release in my spirit and a reuniting of my relationship with God; also absolute victory over the devil. Satan cannot stand for us to praise God, and when this weapon is used in the offensive posture, it can storm the gates of hell.

Christ states, ". . . The gates of hell shall not prevail against it." What a promise! So as Peter was a *chip off the old block*, so are our rights as Christians to be able to come against the bondage of all hell. Whether it be in the lives of people or in circumstances, we can demand that it leave. Our authority is the victory of the cross, for through it we have the word of faith and the blood of Christ. Herein lies our power.

How tragic for the Christian today to be caught
under his circumstances and to have the problems
that he has! I am reminded of a statement made to
me about circumstances and one's being under them
—"What are you doing under there?" Circumstances are piles of wiles brought by the devil to be
heaped over the hearts of Christians. He does this to
bring such heaviness that they are unable to run the
race. They are encumbered, distraught, discouraged
and in despair.

As we study further in the area of prayer being
warfare, again I would like to show you that it is
Christ that must do business with the devil. We cannot do it ourselves for we do not have the power. We
may want to offensively come against the devil in our
carnal state, but we will fail, and in the lost state it is
a dangerous thing to do business with the devil.
There is no power to resist him. This fact was brought
home to us Scripturally in the account of the sons of
Skevia. How tragic today that witchcraft is running as
rampant as it is! People foolishly play games, such as
the ouija board, and other things that are on the
market today. They do not understand that upon
participating in these games they have made contact
with the spirit world. In doing so, they have opened
their bodies to demonic intervention or possession.
With it comes many things such as fear, as spoken of
in II Timothy 1:7: "For God hath not given us the
spirit of fear; but of power, and of love, and of a
sound mind." Fear is a spirit, and as we have said in
another writing, *Deliverance, the Children's Bread*,
anything you can control is flesh; anything that controls you is spirit. If it is the Holy Spirit, you operate

in God's will; if it is the unholy spirit, then your entire attitude, direction and dimension will be against the purpose of the plan of God in all things. Again there are only two spirits—the Holy Spirit and the unholy spirit. And when you open your life to these so-called harmless situations, you will be bothered by thoughts of lust, feelings of anger, hostility, and fears—meanwhile, never understanding why they confuse the life. The devil is a god spelled with a little g. He has power to do things beyond the reason of man. His powers coming upon this present world scene are not appearing in blackest color. By that I mean they do not come just in the arts of witchcraft and black magic, but today Satan is making his move in the world in the cloth of the church. Christians who operate on feeling, through so-called Christian experiences, are many times doing business with the devil. Yes, a Christian can be demonized. However, Christians cannot be demon possessed. They can receive, as the Scriptures say, another spirit. This is found in II Corinthians 11:4 (KJV):

"For if he that cometh preacheth another Jesus, whom we have not preached, or if you receive another spirit, which ye have not received, or another gospel, which ye have not accepted, ye might well bear with him."

Many today are preaching *another Jesus*. They make demands upon the Holy Spirit, commanding Him to do certain things. A favorite verse to back up the demands is found in Isaiah 45:11 (KJV).

"Thus saith the Lord, the Holy One of Israel, and his Maker, Ask me of things to come concerning my sons, and concerning the work of

my hands command ye me."

And yet that verse is parallel to the verse found in I Corinthians 12:11, where the Greek word *bouletai* is used. This verse states:

"But all these worketh that one and the self-same Spirit, dividing to every man severally as he will."

God is emphatic when He states that He chooses as He wills. To bring this together with the verse in Isaiah 45, you will discover that God has a definite plan and purpose for each life. Our position then is to choose God's will for our lives daily. In doing so, Christ may live His life and plan through us. This keeps the Christian from receiving another spirit. The devil wants you to command—rebellion. God says to agree with His will—obedience. Again, in the words of Isaiah, God is saying, "I have a plan for your life. So therefore, choose Me and I will operate that plan through you." For you see, Satan in this end-time, as we mentioned before, is coming not only in the black arts, but he is also coming in the name of Jesus. In II Corinthians 11:13-15, we find:

"For such are false apostles, deceitful workers, transforming themselves into the apostles of Christ.

And no marvel; for Satan himself is transformed into an angel of light.

Therefore it is no great thing if his ministers also be transformed as the ministers of righteousness; whose end shall be according to their works."

Now these are men and women who are false apostles. They will be transforming themselves by great signs and wonders seen visibly by people who would rather have an experience than be crucified (Galatians 2:20). And so these come on the scene doing great miracles by the powers of Satan according to these verses. For Paul says in the 15th verse, ". . . It is no great thing if his ministers be transformed as the ministers of righteousness. . . ." Again the word righteousness means right standing with God. They will look and sound like Jesus Christ. They will perform, in many cases, the miracles of the first century. Now I'm not against miracles. I believe God is showing Himself in this end time in an unusual way. But the Scripture also teaches that Satan is a counterfeit, and a person must be careful when he begins to try to incorporate in his own life the miraculous. The reason is that soul power has a very strong pull from demonic influence. Consequently, when we deal with the devil, we deal with him through the blood of Christ in prayer. That is what warfare is. It is praying in the power of Christ to release, as we have said before, the bondage of Satan in the circumstance of an individual's life. As we have shared in our book, *Deliverance, The Children's Bread*, prayer is the battleground of the mind. Satan's bondage can be broken in any situation even though it looks so insurmountable that it would seem an impossibility. And yet where thousands of people are consumed by demonic influence, one individual in prayer, who is broken and agreeing with God, can actually destroy what the devil has done in their lives. Every great revival in history can be brought back, as you study it, to one individual. We have read of great moves of God in the past where entire populations were changed by the power of God. Each time this can be traced back to one person who was so committed and so broken that he stood in warfare intercession until victory came. Satan's bondage is broken only when a person, in faith, agrees with God's power and flow. And the Scripture teaches that God is looking for that man. His eyes are searching to and fro. Prayer is warfare; prayer breaks the dominions of Satan. It destroys the demonic influence, the hindrances, and renders powerless the effects of the demons who are running more rampant in these end-times. Thank God they are already defeated!

I have talked to others who are excited about what is going on. They still believe in God for a vision and God shares with them what He desires for them to do. And from that vision they are able to believe God and move into the place of power. The Bible teaches that where there is no vision, the people perish. Every great work begun and blessed of God, whether it be church or para-church organization, that is doing an end time ministry for Jesus Christ can be traced back to the vision of one man. He heard from God and tenaciously held on to the promise that was given him. The great churches in history can be traced back to the vision of one man— a pastor who saw what God wanted to do and began to set about in agreement with God's plan for his life. Agreeing with God breaks the bonds of Satan; devastates him; destroys him; reduces him. The prayer warrior who operates in the glory and in the victory knows beyond the shadow of a doubt that the devil is a defeated enemy. He acts like it; he sounds like it; he lives like it; he prays like it. That is the kind of individual that gets things done. For God is able to flow through that person's life to break the mind. Satan is forever moving upon the mind to devastate it and destroy it. In II Corinthians 10:3-5, we find that God states:

> *"For though we walk in the flesh, we do not war after the flesh:*
>
> *(For the weapons of our warfare are not carnal, but mighty through God to the pulling down of strong holds;)*
>
> *Casting down imaginations, and every high thing that exalteth itself against the knowledge of God, and bringing into captivity every thought to the obedience of Christ;"*

Here we find that though we physically live in the flesh, we cannot carry on the warfare according to the flesh. It is an impossibility. I cannot deal with Satan from a carnal posture. It must be Jesus Christ through me defeating the devil. When Satan contends with me as he is doing constantly, my only hope is for him to see about me the glory of God—that I walk in the Spirit. If I retain that posture daily by fully committing my life to Jesus and by constantly being filled with the Spirit as said in Ephesians 5:18, then his power is limited to the level of my commitment to Christ. Satan is defeated in his effort to devastate and destroy my life and separate me from my power and victory. However, before completely covering these verses in II Corinthians 10, let me show you that our power is in Jesus Christ. Once you see this position, then you will understand how to overcome the strongholds that Satan has cast toward the mind—the battleground of the soul. In Ephesians 6:10, Paul, by inspiration, simply says to the church at Ephesus that they must be strong in the Lord and in the power of God's might. Now the strength that He is speaking about here is not the physical stamina of the human body, but it has to do with spiritual strength. Satan in his *wiles*, is constantly draining the spiritual person. He wants him to be carnal and dead. To understand the principle in Ephesians 6 is to comprehend by revelation what is being said, and that is that we are in a constant warfare, and in order to win, we must realize that the battle is the Lord's. It is His battle. It is His fight. I initiate His power by the catalyst of my confession, of not only the sin in my life, but that I desire Him to consume me, control me, to fill me and to live in and through my life. Again, when the devil has to do business with Jesus, he would rather not do business at all. He wants to do business with you. He wants to break the spirit down and devastate it, especially the Christian's life. You see, man was made in the image of God. Satan has already lost the battle in heaven and been cast down upon this earth. Demons today will admit that their time is short. And so, positionally, the way for Satan and demons to get back at God is to move upon His image, man. They hate man and use man as their source of flow and power. They dwell within him and about him constantly, bringing conflict within his person— as spirits of lying, of murder, and of death. As we come to the close of history, we find the devil more rampant today. He is constantly breaking spiritual values. Because of compromise, the Christian's mind is constantly absorbing filth—that is now supposedly the normal condition of human existence. Television, a constant flow of adulterous garbage, is one of the means he uses to punch holes in the soul to let

God's Spirit drain out. Books and magazines that twenty years ago would have been sold under the counter are now being sold on the shelves of our stores. As the people of the world become more and more liberalized in their attitudes, so they continue to die. In regard to this, a well-known evangelist made this statement about America that was so evidently true. He was speaking regarding the sin of this nation and especially the area of homosexuality. His statement was: "If God allows America to survive in the way that it is going, He will have to apologize to Sodom and Gomorrah." The attack on the mind in this, the most perverted of all attacks of demon possession, is now being received as a normal circumstance in the lives of people. I have dealt with homosexuals for years, and I have found them the most miserable, unhappy, vile or violent people I have ever met in my life—totally degraded, completely perverted, especially when they have come to the place spoken of in Romans 1, to where they no longer want to retain God in their knowledge. And yet I have seen warfare praying break the bondage of these Godless people to bring them to the place that they could at least discern that they had a deep spiritual need and get help. Paul, when he spoke to the church at Corinth, made the statement: "Such were some of you." We know that there were converted homosexuals in Corinth who were brought to liberty from this mental disease of demonic control.

And so in Ephesians 6, we find that in order to do battle with the devil, we must put on His might, His power, His authority. Satan is defeated by the person of Jesus Christ. Therefore, if you, as a Christian, are living defeated, it means that you have taken the

Christ in you, and have chosen to let your carnal will overcome His plan for your life, thereby living under your circumstance set up by wiles. How tragic! No victory, no joy, no answered prayer—defeated! However, you can turn this circumstance around by praising Christ in your defeat. This will change the course of your direction. You see the best praying you will ever do is from the posture of brokenness. That is why the greatest thing that can happen to the Christian is to be broken. It is at that time he gets honest with God. When he has the deepest needs, he does his most important praying.

In Ephesians 6, we are commanded to put on the person of Christ constantly. Here it is spoken of as being the whole armor. Because the battle is the Lord's, in order to overcome the devil in warfare praying we must dress up in Him. The reason for this is the reference to *wiles of the devil.* To further explain this, let me say that Satan knows basically how an individual will act in a given circumstance. Because of his position through principalities, he knows what makes him angry, or how to bring lust to the mind. He knows everything about you. No, he is not omnipresent, omniscient, or omnipotent. He cannot be all places at all times. I do not believe he can see into the mind or influence the mind by being in it. But the devil, because he has his whole kingdom set up in principalities, is in communication constantly with these demon forces. Principalities, as we will see in the next verse, are kingdoms here in this world. There is a prince over every nation, a demon spirit who is in control of all the other demon spirits under him. We find this doctrine when Daniel was praying. Twenty-one days from the time he began to pray, the

Archangel, Michael, appeared on the scene and said, "Daniel, your prayer was answered twenty-one days ago, but the Prince of Persia hindered me."

In this we see that over every nation there is a prince. I believe over every city is identically the same thing. I believe over every area is a prince structure and underneath this prince are demon forces of lesser authority who give answer to these areas. In the human body of the demonized person there will always be one dominant spirit in charge. It could be anger, it could be fear, it could be lust, or it could be uncontrolled emotions that, when pursued in that uncontrollable state, make the individual later wonder how he could ever have done anything like he did. For you see, the devil, in setting up his principalities, is constantly working on every individual to remove him from the will of God. And when a Christian becomes a prayer threat to the demonic intervention of another person's life or circumstances, Satan then begins to try to set up circumstances of defeat in that individual's life. We are in a warfare. To overcome this move of Satan, God says that we must in everything give thanks, for God knows of the wiles. Also, Satan knows exactly what to do to stop your spiritual progress. I sometimes call it basketball Christianity— high one moment; low the next—high on Sunday and then as you start the apex of that victory, suddenly the devil moves out in front of you after having backed away for awhile and you think everything is great! "I'm FREE!" Only to find that immediately, Satan sets up a situation for you to fall into his trap, thereby losing your spiritual cool as spoken of in Proverbs 17:27 (AMP).

*"He who has knowledge spares his words, and
a man of understanding has a cool spirit."*

This in turn brings a separation from God's control
as you react from the carnal nature and suddenly find
yourself flat on your face in your spiritual position.
The principalities have won again, and the threat to
Satan's dominions is no longer existing. You are discouraged, despondent and in despair, and wonder
why that everytime you get started with God, something happens. To enter into warfare praying is to
break these kinds of bondages. It must be understood
that the devil is a roaring lion seeking whom he may
devour. He is working out circumstances constantly
to keep the Christian bound and defeated. In the
verse we find, "For we wrestle not against flesh and
blood." Another translation says, "For we are not
fighting against people made of flesh and blood, but
against persons without bodies—the evil rulers of the
unseen world." Years ago I was fascinated by a mov-
ie called, "The Invisible Man." I often wondered
where a person could go, what he could do and what
he could see if he were invisible. As a child I fanta-
sized experiences. To be able to be present and parti-
cipate without anyone's knowledge would be unique.
Such is the case of human existence at this period of
history. There are persons about us now. There are
invisible beings that are about or in us at this present
moment. They usually enter through the mouth and
rein and dwell within the human physical body.
They attach themselves as leeches upon the living.
They are filthy and perverted. A number of years ago
we dealt with a woman who was very attractive and
showed her beauty with as much exposure of her

physical body as she possibly could. These were the days of the micro-mini skirts and low-cut blouses. She came to a service, and during that service God broke her heart. After the service was over we prayed with her, and as we were praying, her voice changed to a high pitch. At that moment we came face to face with a spirit whose name was vanity. Suddenly, this woman's face contorted and as it did, I simply asked the spirit what right it had to stay in her life.

It screamed back at me, "I make her pretty, I make her pretty."

Taking authority in prayer, I demanded that Satan's bondage be broken and that the spirit would be bound from this woman's life.

Suddenly her countenance changed, and as she began to weep, she prayed her way into the Kingdom of God upon confession of sin and inviting Jesus Christ into her heart. She was born again!

The next night she came to the service and her dress was different. She had on what was the opposite of that present day naked exposure of human flesh. She had on a granny dress. It was a beautiful, old fashioned, long dress. It had a high collar that was tied with a black ribbon. It had long sleeves that were cuffed with a black ribbon. During the testimony time before the service began, this beautiful woman whose countenance was radiant with the Glory of God upon it, stood and stated that within the last twenty-four hour period she had had the greatest victory she had ever known in her life.

She confessed an inward gentleness, joy and peace that she had never experienced before. She then said, "But, Brother Bonner, I cannot seem to get enough clothes on since I had this experience."

One of the evident signs of demon possession or demonization is the need to expose the physical body. This is noticed in the prostitute as well as the homosexual. There is a must to expose the physical. They are captured. Again the Scripture says, ''For we wrestle not against flesh and blood.'' Warfare praying is breaking the dominions and the wiles that Satan has overcome in a circumstance in a person's life. Now to do that, we must bring to Satan, not ourselves, but Jesus Christ. It is imperative that we dress in the armor of God. Again that armor is Christ, for Ephesians 6:10-13 tells us if we do not dress in the armor of God, we cannot stand against the wiles of the devil. That means that Satan knows so much about us, that no matter what we do, he can overcome us, unless we submit to Jesus Christ and let Him deal directly with Satan.

God tells us in His Word to overcome the wiles, and to be able to do so, we must have our loins girded about with truth. The loins were girded with a leather band that not only held the breast plate tightly, but also held the sword. In this case truth is Jesus Christ. We must have truth in the inward parts. Jesus Christ said, ''I am the way, the truth and the life.'' Therefore, in order to present an offensive posture to the devil, we are to be girded in truth. Satan will know when we are. Furthermore, we must have on the breastplate of righteousness, the covering of the chest area. Then when we encounter demonic dominions, they deal directly with Christ. Righteousness means right standing with God. This means that Satan looks at us to try to set up wiles to destroy or defeat our relationship. He sees that we stand in righteousness, which is Christ. At that point, he is already defeated.

Now we are commanded to have our feet shod with the preparation of the Gospel of Peace. Who was the Prince of Peace? Jesus Christ. Look at John 14:27:

> *"Peace I leave with you, my peace I give unto you: not as the world giveth, give I unto you. Let not your heart be troubled, neither let it be afraid."*

Who is our peace? It is Jesus. We live at the level of peace to the extent that Christ controls our lives. Frustration is the seed of Satan. Mental conflict is the after effect of the circumstance of wiles. The person who operates in grace, operates in peace. The individual who has that peace is totally quieted within himself. Even standing in the midst of death, it holds no sting. And so when our feet are shod with the preparation of the Gospel of Peace, we find ourselves in Him. He is the ". . . Lamp to our feet, the light to our path." He is our ". . . Path of righteousness . . ." and then comes the statement, "Above all, taking the shield of faith . . ." (Ephesians 6:16). Who is our faith? We are commanded to live by the faith of the Son of God. It is by His faith that we know we can storm the strongholds of hell. ". . . The gates of hell shall not prevail . . ." is our promise. Those things that Satan has set up are overcome by His power, so we live at the level of faith to the extent that Christ controls our lives. The shield is Christ Himself.

Now here is how Christ will use Himself as an instrument of our faith. He states that with that shield we will be able to quench all the fiery darts of the wicked. How beautiful! You see, if you are in a defensive posture, you are over in the corner cowed down behind your armor, hoping that when these darts come, they will not hit you, but your armor. But you have to understand that the devil is subtle, street-wise and smart. He can get you from behind. If you will notice, the armor is designed to be worn only one way, and that only covers the front. It is used totally in the offensive posture. Again, when the shield is used in faith, the devil is defeated.

Now we come to a new weapon of war—the helmet of salvation. In this case the helmet of salvation is the mind of God. Who is our salvation? Jesus Christ. So therefore, when we place the mind of Christ (Philippians 2:5) over ours, we think with His mind. You see, our ways are not His ways, and our thoughts are not His thoughts, so to enter into the battlefield of prayer, or warfare praying, we must do it from His mental level. To receive His direction or will, we place the helmet of salvation, or in this case, the mind of God, over our minds. We have taken the posture of Romans 12:2 (KJV):

"And be not conformed to this world: but be ye transformed by the renewing of your mind, that ye may prove what is that good, and acceptable, and perfect, will of God."

Then we are told to take up the sword of the Spirit. Who is the sword? As a play on the word sword, if you take away the "s," you have the truth of the statement, for Jesus is the Word. We could then add the letter, s, to mean that the Word used in the Spirit is a weapon of offense to overcome Satan and his demonic powers. I have known those who have prayed Scriptures, claiming their positions and thereby using God's Word as an instrument of warfare for overcoming the devil. It works! Again, used in this manner, Christ is in you, the hope of glory. It is the fullness of the Godhead bodily, and so therefore when we take that sword of the Spirit, which is the Word of God, and offensively approach the devil, he is defeated. Again, the Word of God is Jesus Christ. For in John 1:1-2 (KJV) it states:

> *"In the beginning was the Word, and the Word was with God, and the Word was God. The same was in the beginning with God."*

In John 1:14 (KJV) we find:

> *"And the Word was made flesh, and dwelt among us, (and we beheld his glory, the glory as of the only begotten of the Father,) full of grace and truth."*

Who is the Word? It is Jesus. I don't mean to repeat this, but the Christian must know the power of the Word. Then when we take the sword and offensively approach the devil, who is he seeing? Jesus. When he sees us dressed like or with Christ, Satan knows he is defeated and he runs, or to use a Scripture word, *flees.* Therefore, when we pray we must be totally committed, completely yielded, absolutely filled with the person of Jesus Christ. For you see, as stated before, the battlefield is prayer; the battleground is the mind.

SPIRIT PRAYING

In Ephesians 6:18, the Scripture teaches,

> *"Praying always with all prayer and supplica-*

tion in the Spirit, and watching thereunto with all perseverance and supplication for all saints;''

How are we to pray? In the Spirit. Who is our authority? Jesus. Who is our power? Jesus. Where is the battleground? It is the mind. So who are we to fill our minds with? Jesus! Now let us go back to II Corinthians 10 (AMP), to show you how to tear down the strongholds of the mind. In the third verse, as we shared at the outset of this chapter, God states:

"For though we walk in the flesh, we are not carrying on our warfare according to the flesh and using mere human weapons.''

Satan is a subtle enemy in that he knows how to devastate the individual Christian's walk. The person who walks in less than the level of a Spirit-filled, controlled relationship with Christ will not be effective in the conflict against strongholds. Therefore, Satan will do all he possibly can to keep his presence unknown, but if he becomes known, then he will move the pendulum to the other side and try to get that person's mind constantly upon him. This is the case of many Christians who have gone from the darkness of having just a little knowledge of their enemy to being overboard and back into bondage by dwelling too much on Satan and demons. The Christian who cannot conduct warfare is living in a carnal relationship, and the one who constantly dwells on the demonic is also placed in that carnal position because, unless Jesus Christ has captured the mind and controls it completely, that person will become transfixed with spiritual warfare. He sees a demon in everything. The priority of the Christian's life must be

Jesus Christ. Our commitment must be fully to Him. These verses are emphatic in their position of the teaching of carnal relationships. What is a carnal Christian? As Manley Beasley states, "It is a Christian that has received light and rejected it." For the most part, our churches today are bound by carnal nature. The business of the kingdom is run by the level of men's mentality rather than by God's revelation. That is why, when something supernatural and of God does come along, the average Christian of today does not know how to handle it. Therefore, he tacks a label on it. He states that either he doesn't understand it or it's not the doctrine of his denomination.

Looking further into II Corinthians 10:3, we see that God says if we walk in the flesh we do not war after the flesh. The meaning of this is that if we are carnal we are already defeated. The devil is in control and we are bound. No carnal Christian will ever effectively pray. In a later chapter we will cover the verse that states, ". . . The effective, fervent prayer of a righteous man availeth much" (James 5:16). Righteousness in the Word of God means right standing with God. Therefore, to do battle with the devil, we must so live in the armor that it is Christ who is coming against the devil. Or, to turn it around, if we are obedient to Jesus, He will place us in the right posture so that He, through us, can bring down the strongholds. The carnal Christian is already defeated. What constitutes carnality? Well, Paul had a great deal of problems with the Corinthian church and he called them carnal. We find this in I Corinthians 3:1, where Paul says:

"And I, brethren, could not speak unto you as unto spiritual, but as unto carnal, even as unto babes in Christ."

Several things are found here to show that they were not in warfare. Number one, he said they were not spiritual. Now to be spiritual is to be Spirit-controlled, Spirit-filled, Spirit-led—captured by Christ in a day by day encounter, relinquishing our lives to Him, that He might, through us, be Himself, and that the world in seeing us might turn its face to Him, saying, "I believe." This position has already been established in us at our new birth.

"I am crucified with Christ: nevertheless I live; yet not I, but Christ liveth in me: and the life which I now live in the flesh I live by the faith of the Son of God, who loved me, and gave himself for me."

(Galatians 2:20, KJV)

This word carnal, in I Corinthians 3:1, is from the Greek word *Sarkainos*, which means flesh or fleshly, or better said, what a man is more prone to do in the flesh. For example, he is more prone to relate to all circumstances, not from the spiritual aspect, but from the reasoning aspect—no revelation; just reason. So in that first verse, Paul says they were carnal, and as always is the case, the way to tell if a church is carnal is that it desires a milk message rather than a meat message. A baby in Christ in the local church would rather have his pastor preach to him how to be born again, than to preach to him how to be broken, crucified and resurrected in Christ. Paul states in the second verse that he had fed them with milk and not with meat. Now again, meat is the message of commitment; milk is the message of salvation. When you begin to preach commitment to a carnal Christian, he begins to choke. To the carnal Christian, when the salvation message is preached, it does not bring judgment upon his life that in turn brings conviction to the way he is living. In fact, Paul says in the second verse that they were not able to bear the meat. Then Paul in the third verse of that chapter again uses the word carnal, but this time it is used as an adverb, which simply means fleshly or these people were living like lost men. They were living like the world. If you have to change your attitude or your language as you go from your car to the church, it is very evident that you are carnal and have no power in the position of warfare praying. God, through Paul, emphasizes this strongly in this verse. He says the way to tell if you are carnal is if you have envy and strife and divisions in your heart toward others. Now we have already covered the Scriptures that teach if you have anything in your heart against another person, you do not have one prayer answered. Therein lies the reason our churches, for the most part, are dead today. They have no power in prayer. There is no brokenness or commitment in Christians. In order to have revival, churches try to bring in a known personality. They feel, for the most part, that in his coming he will draw crowds, thereby showing evidence of God's moving. God says we must get on our knees or our faces before God and travail in fasting and prayer for revival.

"If my people, which are called by my name, shall humble themselves, and pray, and seek

*my face, and turn from their wicked ways; then
will I hear from heaven, and will forgive their
sin, and will heal their land.''*

We acquaint revival with the numbers that come
down the aisle (in most churches). But revival is when
people have faced themselves, based on the teaching
of the Word of God, and rejected what they are and
cry out to God. They see the wretchedness of their
persons and then are broken. That is revival! Always
on the wings of that kind of experience will come a
great move of the Spirit of God that will have an
eternal reckoning, not only in the church, but in that
community. Incidentally, as was mentioned earlier,
if you study revival you can always trace it back to one
individual who, in brokenness, paid the price through
prayer until finally the strongholds of Satan were broken and the prince and power of the air was bound
back. Then God's holiness poured out in glory—not
just mercy drops, but showers of blessing. However,
if one has envy and strife and divisions, he is carnal.
You see, to have envy in the heart is to be completely
separated from God's will and devastated by the devil. If there is strife in the heart or negative feelings
toward another individual, living or dead, it means
being bound to Satan's camp.

It may be that you are saved; however, you are in a
defensive posture. In other words, you are saying,
''Satan, if you will leave me alone, I'll leave you
alone.'' Again, that was actually said to me ten years
prior to this writing by a pastor who knew that we
were teaching spiritual warfare. His statement was,
''I made a pact with the devil—if he would leave me
alone, I would leave him alone.'' This is not criti-

cism. But looking at this precious man's ministry you can see they both kept their bargain. God was ushered out of the picture. However, the person who enters into warfare praying will move to great victory. In fact, there will never be revival without it. Until we are able to contend by prayer with the bondage of Satan in a person's life or circumstance, we will never see real victory.

In a recent meeting I conducted, there were two churches attending. In the course of a message I felt led to say of those two churches that the one that learned and used warfare praying would be the one to contend with Satan by bringing down his strongholds, thereby bringing revival to that city. And this is so. Again, what hinders revival? Carnal flesh. I am amazed how Satan has bound our churches today. In selecting men for leadership positions in the church, people are chosen, not for their quality in positional praying, but for their ability in the mental aspects to cope, usually with financial decisions and positions. God help the church that selects men based on their ability of business rather than their relationship to brokenness! The devil enjoys conducting the church's business. Again, as Revelation 3 states, the churches of the Laodicean age will be carnal. For in the body there is envy, strife and divisions (I Corinthians 3:3). Look at the word, division. It means that if there is one individual in a service that is upset with another individual, the Spirit of God is quenched. How many times has God desired to do a work among the brethren, but within that body of believers collected and assembled would be negative feelings engineered by Satanic atmospheric dominion just before their arrival at the service? Whether it be husband and wife,

parents and children, or one individual upset with
another individual in the congregation, it must be
realized that this devastates and destroys what God is
desiring to do. The Amplified Bible states that they
walk as mere unchanged men (I Corinthians 3:3).
God then declares that they are not under spiritual
authority. He says that one is of Paul and another of
Apollos (I Corinthians 3:4). What does he mean? Everybody has a pastor. It might be the one that is there
at the moment; it may be one they have known in
past years; but everybody has a favorite pastor. Such
was the case in Corinth. Some of the body loved Paul
and his deep teachings. Others loved Apollos and his
great ability to preach the Word in depth and quality. But have you noticed, Paul makes no mention of
the pastor that was over the church at the time? Now
we have covered this in another book, but I am going
to share it with you in part at this time. If you are not
under pastoral covering and authority, then you are
openly subject to Satanic dominion over everything
that you do. The Christian must have covering. This
is strongly emphasized in Ephesians 4:11-16. Also, it
is mentioned in I Peter 5:1-5. You also find this teaching in Hebrews 13:7. God is emphatic about spiritual
authority. We must have covering. This places us in
the right relationship with God in order for the devil's strongholds to be broken in the Christian's life.
God states through Paul in Romans 8:6:

> *"For to be carnally minded is death; but to be
> spiritually minded is life and peace."*

That, more simply put, means if we do not have Holy Spirit revelation, we cannot live the spiritual life;
thus there is no warfare. He gives the reason for this

in the seventh verse. We find that the carnal mind is enmity against God; for it is not subject to the law of God, neither indeed can be. Now hold on to this— the mind that is fleshly or carnal is hostile toward God. It does not want to yield itself to God. Again, how many times has God begun to do a work that would be spiritual and moving in a church, when suddenly, carnal men rise up and shut the door to it, and say, "That's not," and then they would quote their denomination? Another translation says the carnal mind is hostile to God. Romans 8:8 states:

"So then they that are in the flesh cannot please God."

Why? Because they are controlled by a spirit. It is not the Holy Spirit; it is the unholy spirit. Oh, they want to be led of the Spirit, they want to walk in the Spirit, but they want to pull God's string and make Him dance to their needs. In fact, God is so emphatic in this that lust enters into the picture. Now in Galatians 5:16-17 the Scripture states:

"This I say then, Walk in the Spirit, and ye shall not fulfil the lust of the flesh.
For the flesh lusteth against the Spirit, and the Spirit against the flesh: and these are contrary the one to the other: so that ye cannot do the things that ye would."

(KJV)

Now in the 16th verse we are commanded to walk in the Spirit and not to fulfil the lust of the flesh. In this case, what is lust? Lust is something that consumes one, based on a want in one's own spirit or person. The common vernacular refers to sexual perversion. However said, it is still a consuming desire within the heart. For God says that the flesh does lust after the spirit. Again, what does it mean? The carnal flesh would like to have the Spirit around when it needs it. But it does not want to pay the price of submission. It would rather live in subjection to Satanic dominion than in the flow of God's Spirit. However, when a person has been broken and moved to the relationship of fulness, to what a joyous level he participates! He wonders, as I have many times, why he has rejected God's Spirit in his life. The happiest moments in life are those in the midst of God's plan and purpose for the life. God says that carnal flesh lusteth against the spirit. But also in that verse it says the spirit lusteth against the flesh. What does that mean? It is God's desire not only to consume and control you, but also to bring you to the victory of His life, which is found in Galatians 5:22-26 (AMP).

"But the fruit of the (Holy) Spirit, (the work which His presence within accomplishes)—is love, joy (gladness), peace, patience (an even temper, forbearance), kindness, goodness (benevolence), faithfulness; (Meekness, humility) gentleness, self-control (self-restraint, continence). Against such things there is no law (that can bring a charge).

And those who belong to Christ Jesus, the Messiah, have crucified the flesh—the Godless human nature—with its passions and appetites and desires.

If we live by the (Holy) Spirit, let us also walk by the Spirit. If by the (Holy) Spirit we

> *have our life (in God), let us go forward walking in line, our conduct controlled by the Spirit.*
>
> *Let us not become vainglorious and self-conceited, competitive and challenging and provoking and irritating to one another, envying and being jealous of one another."*

God's purpose is to bring down strongholds in your life through warfare praying. He desires to do battle with the enemy through you as a vessel of His grace. God lusts in His Spirit to consume your spirit. He cries out, "Oh, why don't you let me have control?" Why won't you; why don't you? We cannot enter into the spiritual warfare doing the works of the flesh, but only by the flow of the Spirit. Prayer is warfare. If Satan has dominion in our hearts and we operate in carnal flesh, there is no answer to prayer. For as we have shared before in II Corinthians 10, He literally commands us not to walk in the flesh. We are not to be carnal. But he also shares that if we are, we are defeated.

Let's look again at Paul's statement in II Corinthians 10:4. Here it is declared, "For the weapons of our warfare are not carnal, but mighty through the pulling down of strongholds" (KJV). Now in this is the statement that we do have weapons. And not only are the weapons in the present tense, but also warfare is in the present tense. We are, at this moment, in a battle. Christians are in a constant never-ceasing conflict. Again the battlefield is prayer; the battleground, our minds. When we understand that we are at war with the devil and that he is making a move to consume and overcome us, the results will then be life-changing! Satan must keep us blinded to his person, personality or purpose, and in that blindness, we tend to call our conflicts or strongholds, circumstances; however, these circumstances are engineered. In this case, Satan, through his wiles, is constantly creating a crisis to keep the Christian devastated, destroyed, in despair, or for the most part, discouraged. You see, you must understand that prayer in the life of the Christian is not defensive posture, but it is an offensive posture. The Christian who is constantly trying to build his defenses to keep Satan away is already defeated. There is no place in the Word of God where he is to take that defensive part. In faith we are to be aggressive. The Bible says we are to ''. . . Live by the faith of the Son of God. . . .'' Faith is the activity of the soul taking God at His Word and confessing a thing as if it is already done. Prayer is the same way. Prayer is an aggressive posture of the Christian pulling down strongholds that Satan has set up in the life or in a circumstance. We have the right to storm the gates of hell. They will not prevail. They will not remain. They will not stand. We have the right as Christians to run at those gates demanding that Satan's bondage be broken and that he must turn loose of that which he controls. But the Christian who is over in the corner tending his wound can rest assured that when that one begins to heal, the devil shall inflict another, thereby keeping him a casualty. We are in a battle; we are in a conflict. We have weapons and we are to be aggressive in the position of using those weapons; we are to crash into that course of events where the dominion of Satan is the strongest. We are to take authority and in agreement with God, we energize that which is already bound and loosed in heaven to be bound and loosed here upon this earth (Matthew 18:18). Then as we come in an aggressive move toward Satan's dominion, just before we arrive in faith, the strongholds are broken. Satan and demons cannot stand against the glory of God. Therefore, the Christian dressed in the armor of God (Jesus), with the sword (Word) extended and the shield (faith) in its place, running toward Satan's gates, shall find them breeched before arriving. The course is then to climb on the rubble and shout the victory. I think this was vividly illustrated to us in Joshua's move around the walls of Jericho. They marched on that last day seven times around. They remained quiet until, as instructed, they turned and faced those walls. They shouted and blew those ram horns. What did it mean? It meant that they shouted the victory before they entered the battle. And upon shouting, the battle became the Lord's; then the strongholds or the walls came down, and they climbed the rubble, moved in and took possession. That is the kind of God I serve. And when you learn that Satan is a defeated enemy, that he was defeated at Calvary and that in the very presence of Christ he quakes, you will learn to begin to move in such sovereign glory and victory that your ministry will cease to be that of guesswork and become that of a stalwart soldier standing ". . . Fast therefore in the liberty wherewith Christ hath made us free" (Galatians 5:1). There is no greater experience in life than through prayer to move toward the bastions of hell, shatter their dominions and watch the captives liberated! Here is answered prayer. Again, Paul says, "For the weapons of our warfare are not physical (weapons of flesh and blood) but they are mighty before God for the overthrow and destruction of strongholds.'' The key to it is the word, through. Number one, we have weapons; number two, we are in warfare; and number three, the power that we have is through God. Again, when you move in prayer toward the bastions of Satan, he does not see you; he sees God. He is defeated in the presence of God. That is why nothing is insurmountable. When faced through the eyes of God and through the will of God, there is no one so bound by Satan that those bonds cannot be broken! There is nothing so overwhelming that, once positioned in the will of God, those areas cannot be shattered! The devil is defeated! He will act defeated when he is approached by a committed prayer warrior.

DYNAMITE

Salvation does not work like that. New Testament new birth only comes to the sinner who has seen himself as he really is. It comes when he has abhorred what he has seen and, in rejecting it, cries out for Jesus Christ as his personal savior. His desperation was as a drowning man dying in the water, going down, until the last strength was gone from his body and with one maximum effort he screamed, ''Save me!'' True repentance comes on the wings of that kind of revelation. And that revelation comes as an illumination of sin in one's life when an individual stands in the presence, spiritually, of the Lord Jesus Christ and sees himself as he really is and recognizes he is a sinner. Now who wants to hide that? Who wants to veil that? The devil. He does such a good job that the Gospel, the Good News of Jesus Christ, the Messiah, Who is the image and likeness of God, cannot shine to these people. You say, "What is the answer?" Very simple. Warfare praying. What you are to do under a burden for that individual's soul is to contend with the devil. First break out of the carnal position of your own life, thereby knowing that the weapons of your warfare are not carnal. Then move in with the dunamis of the Gospel, and thereby blast out the strongholds of Satan. In other words, dunamis means dynamite, and, Dear Friend, there is no stronghold that can stand in the presence of the dynamite of the Word of God that comes through the piercing position of a broken heart believing God for victory. Again, you see, the weapons of our warfare are not carnal but mighty through God to the pulling down of strongholds. What is answered prayer? It is God's flow through our lives; God's power and purpose, each propagating itself through our persons when we are placed in the position of His perfect will. Another way to say it is to live in such a way that we find out by intuitive revelation what is bound and loosed in Heaven and declare it so. How can I have this? How can I enter into warfare praying? Well, the price is your mind! The cost is to be so broken over what you are that you cry out in desperation for what He is! In II Corinthians 10:5, the Scripture says:

"Casting down imaginations, and every high thing that exalteth itself against the knowledge of God, and bringing into captivity every thought to the obedience of Christ;"

(KJV)

What is a condition of warfare praying? It is complete and absolute yieldedness of our lives to Jesus Christ—so much so that we will know the difference between our thoughts and His thoughts. You see, before God can interject His thoughts or His will to us, our minds must be in the position to be receptive to them. We must volitionally choose to bring down strongholds in our own lives so that we can, by His grace, flow and move into a posture of revelation. The world has yet to see what can happen through the life of one person committed totally to Christ. That, more simply put, would be that history has yet to see what one person (so desperately in love with Jesus) could do in the crucifying of his life and committing of his person to Christ daily that He could perform through him His unique plan of prayer. Some have touched it. History records the events that came through their commitment—not that they wanted recognition, but because the world was awestruck by it. But what happened through their relationship with Christ? Again every great revival in history can be traced back to its beginning roots to one person's praying. I am reminded of the story of Rees Howells, whose life was so committed to Christ that he was able to turn the tide of the Second World War as far as England was concerned. Winston Churchill's statement was, "England owed her victory to the prayers of a man, and that man was Rees Howells." Do you want to enter into warfare praying? Do you want pure victory in your life? Then I urge you to cast down imaginations. Throw away anything that is in your life that exalts itself against the knowledge of God. No matter what it is, throw it down. Ask God to reveal yourself to you as He sees you. When this happens, you will begin to break through. You will break those strongholds that bind you so deeply. Every thought will be brought into captivity, every negative thing thrown at you by Satan will be covered with praise and overcome through prayer. You will be released. God will bring the victory, and the devil will be defeated. You must be broken. For again in the amplified translation of this verse we find that God says, ". . . Every proud and lofty thing that sets itself up against the true knowledge of God . . ." must be broken. ". . . We lead every thought and purpose away captive into the obedience of Christ, the Messiah, the Anointed One." When we do that we then enter into the position of revelation where we can actually find the mind of God. When we get home someday we will discover that the greatest soldier in history in the battle with the devil will be the individual who was so yielded to God that he constantly walked in victory. The victory is that he had the mind of Christ and believed it and confessed it, and in so doing, destroyed the works of the devil. Every born again believer can and is commanded by God to enter into that position. Not to do so is to be carnal-minded; or better said, dead; hostile to God. Do you have answered prayer?

CHAPTER THREE

THE REAL MEANING OF THE LORD'S PRAYER

"Take heed that ye do not your alms before men, to be seen of them: otherwise ye have no reward of your Father which is in heaven.

Therefore when thou doest thine alms, do not sound a trumpet before thee, as the hypocrites do in the synagogues and in the streets, that they may have glory of men. Verily I say unto you, They have their reward.

But when thou doest alms, let not thy left hand know what thy right hand doeth:

That thine alms may be in secret: and thy Father which seeth in secret himself shall reward thee openly.

And when thou prayest, thou shalt not be as the hypocrites are: for they love to pray standing in the synagogues and in the corners of the streets, that they may be seen of men. Verily I say unto you, They have their reward.

But thou, when thou prayest, enter into thy closet, and when thou hast shut the door, pray to thy Father which is in secret; and thy Father which seeth in secret shall reward thee openly. But when ye pray, use not vain repetitions, as the heathen do: for they think that they shall be heard for their much speaking.

Be not ye therefore like unto them; for your Father knoweth what things ye have need of, before ye ask him.

After this manner therefore pray ye: Our Father which art in heaven, Hallowed be thy name.

Thy kingdom come. Thy will be done in earth as it is in heaven.

Give us this day our daily bread.

And forgive us our debts, as we forgive our debtors.

And lead us not into temptation, but deliver us from evil: For thine is the kingdom and the power and the glory, for ever. Amen.''

(Matthew 6:1-13 KJV)

Several days ago I stood inside the only church that Mussolini built in the Holy Land. It was erected as a ploy to gain favor for his fascist regime before the Second World War. It is situated on the Sea of Galilee, and is on the Mount of Beatitudes. Of the several places in that land where the overwhelming presence of God is felt, it is here that we have seen so many people meet God in a quiet and unique way. In spite of it being built for propaganda reasons, the atmosphere is saturated with the presence of Christ, because of prayer. This is due mainly to the hundreds who daily visit this site, stopping to pray. It is our procedure when we go with our groups to read to them the Beatitudes from Matthew 5 and 6, emphasizing the so-called Lord's Prayer. How precious the time is in the Word! Then we ask the people to find a quiet place in the gardens and pray. We have seen lives changed at this spot.

It is in this regard that we share this chapter, that we might truly have an insight into what the Lord's Prayer is all about. There are two instances in the Scripture when the Lord's Prayer is given, one in Matthew 6, and the other Luke 11:1-4. It is commonly believed by theologians that these were two separate instances and two different locations. However, basically, both prayers are the same (except for one line). In this case we are dealing with the Lord's Prayer in Matthew 6.

REPETITION

One of the great dangers found in praying is the position of repetition. Even in my own life, I have used the Lord's Prayer as an outlet rather than a power. By that I mean, instead of getting down to business with God in brokenness and truly seeking God's will and mind, I would simply quote the Lord's Prayer in order to release my spiritual obligation to "Pray without ceasing" (I Thessalonians 5:17 KJV). Again, this is a grave danger. We teach our children little rote prayers, which eventually hinder rather than help. How cute to hear a child pray, "Now I lay me down to sleep, I pray the Lord my soul to keep. If I should die before I wake, I pray the Lord my soul to take"; or at the table, at mealtime, "God is great, God is good, Let us thank Him for this food. By His hands we'll all be fed, give us, Lord, our daily bread." How many times as a small child did I hear Grandmother pray that prayer? Consequently, in desperate needs in my life at later times, my whole concept of praying was the reciting of that which I had heard.

Let me urge every Christian parent to teach his children that praying is talking to God. Many times I have used the illustration in sermons that if every time I walked up to you I said, "Hello, how are you? Good to see you; So long," only to meet you at a later time and say, "Hello, how are you? Good to see you; So long," and then upon another chance meeting my greeting to you was, "Hello, how are you? Good to see you; So long." Then one day as you are standing with friends and I walk down the street, you say to your friends, "Do you see that nut? When he gets here he'll say, 'Hello, how are you? Good to see you; So long.' " Sure enough, you are not disappointed; as when I get there I say, "Hello, how are you? Good to see you; So long." You would think something was wrong with me, and you would be right. My intelligence would render me incapable of communicating with any other statement than that which came in my salutation to you. How do you think God feels when we constantly quote a rote prayer? In it there is no brokenness, no meaning, no real position of yieldedness to our lives. Christ spoke of this in His Sermon on the Mount. In fact, He became very adamant regarding how to pray. In Matthew 6:5-8, He deals specifically in the attitude of prayer. He tells us not to be as hypocrites and pray standing in the synagogues or in the corners of the streets to be seen. This is not a negative confession, but how many times have you heard someone called upon to pray, and before he even began (because you have heard it so many times before), you could repeat his general move of not only blessing that begins in the church, but moves to the city, and eventually moves around the world into the mission fields, ending on the same note of unbelief?

I was born again at the age of twenty-three, and after having attended church and Sunday School for several weeks, I suddenly had an overwhelming fear that I might be called upon to pray. I knew I needed to be ready for this event, so to prepare myself, I went to a Christian bookstore. Upon arrival I was greeted and asked if I had a specific need. I shared with a very precious lady, Mrs. Oran, who eventually became a very good friend, that I needed something on prayer. She led me to a shelf filled with books on prayer, and as I began to search I could not find what I needed. She asked again if there was a specific need, and I replied, "Yes, I'm looking for prayers." Her first thought was that I was looking for books on prayer, but when I finally shared with her that I was looking for specific prayers or a prayer book, she led me to the end of the shelf to a little book entitled, *John Wesley's Prayers*. I was thoroughly unfamiliar at that time with any names that were on the edge of these covers, much less the wonderful name of John Wesley. However, when I looked inside, it was exactly what I needed. I purchased it, took it home, and began a sustained reading effort until I found a prayer that wasn't too long or too short. I needed to be ready in case I was ever called on to pray. I memorized this beautiful prayer. In God's divine plan, as He would have it, the next Sunday morning I was called on to pray. As we bowed our heads, I was ready. I began to pray with such eloquence and depth for a new-born child of God that it overwhelmed the Sunday School teacher. He later went to the pastor of the church and said, "You ought to hear Brother Bonner pray." As God would do it, in His own way, he did, for at the end of the service that day, the pastor called on me to pray. It was then that I became aware of the fact that either I needed to memorize a second prayer or maybe prayer was not memorization, but actually speaking from the heart. Herein, again, lies the position as Jesus taught his disciples about prayer. Prayer is simply talking to God about things He wants to hear. We will share later in another chapter on how to find the mind of God, to speak His will in agreement, for again in Matthew 6:5, He states that we are not to pray as the hypocrites, for they love to be seen and heard. God says that they have their reward. He later proclaims in Matthew 6:6, that we are to do closet praying. When we do business with God, we are to be in that relationship of just being alone with Him, whether we are in a crowd or by ourselves.

Again, prayer is focusing in and talking to the Divine Person. Many times I have heard people say, "Well, I just can't pray unless I am on my knees." Please understand, as we stated earlier, it is not the position of the body, but the condition of the heart. It is not where we are or who we are, but simply the soul of man open to the soul of God. For God places His heart upon our hearts; His will upon our lives. We must agree with it. Not only does God place His heart upon us, which is His mind, but He meets us every morning with it.

> *"What is man, that thou shouldest magnify him? and that thou shouldest set thine heart upon him?*
> *And that thou shouldest visit him every morning, and try him every moment?"*
>
> (Job 7:17-18)

Again, prayer is not a position of the body, but a living relationship. God commands us to pray without ceasing. This does not mean to be in a posture upon your knees twenty-four hours a day, but in an attitude of life—holiness being actively manifested through the life of the individual. Prayer is Jesus Christ being Himself through you. Again, let me re-state that—Prayer is simply letting Jesus Christ control our lives constantly; daily. Living prayer is living the abundant life, in constant communication with God's plan and purpose. So in physical praying, it is not just done in public, but more so it should be done in private. There should be a quiet time daily in the life of the individual—a time to study to show himself approved unto God—a time to be alone with the Lord in communication. For the most part we feel it is our speaking to Him, but prayer is actually His speaking to us, as we will see in the chapter on agreeing with God.

In Matthew 6:7, as a preamble to teaching the Lord's Prayer, He states that we are not to use vain repetitions as the heathen do. Such is the case where I meet you on the street with ''Hello—how are you, etc.'' Dear friend, how desperately important this is! Again, it is not the position of the body but the con-dition of the heart. In this case, it is not the volume of words, and their repetition, but the truth that is in the heart being exposed to God. We must under-stand that God not only knows the thoughts of our minds, but he knows the intents of our hearts. He knows who we are and what we are, what we are say-ing and what we really mean when we say it. We can-not fool God. That's why there is so much teaching on the basis of prayer.

Prayer is brokenness, exposed to either praise or need, for praying is simply talking to God about things that He wants to hear—and not from a level of so-called spiritual maturity as we shall see in just a moment. Again, as we look at the verse, the Gentiles or heathen heap their prayers over and over, bombarding Heaven, feeling that by the volume of their words they can enter into the very presence and holiness of God. It reminds me of Elijah's experience as the prophets of Baal and the prophets of the lake, in order to get their god's attention, began to inflict wounds on their bodies, cutting themselves with sharp stones. Elijah's retort to this was, ''He's a god, perhaps he's asleep.'' Our God is not asleep—be honest with Him. Be open to Him—speak your heart. Approach Him in openness. In fact, approach Him as He teaches His disciples to approach Him, in, again, what we call the Lord's Prayer. For the verses preceding the Lord's Prayer began from the negative side, sharing what was not to be done: not to be seen or heard, not to pray in vain repetition, not to be heard for much speaking, repeating a prayer over and over, etc. This does not bring forgiveness, nor does it get the attention of God. Chanting or quoting does not bring his mind to you. Only obedience, brokenness, openness, and longing for His precious presence can create that position in your heart, for He says in the eighth verse that we are not to be like those people who do these things. Why? Because God already knows the needs we have before we ask Him. Therefore, our position is to be in praise. We are commanded to be obedient, yielded, and from that posture our lives become His. God will not give His children stone for bread. In fact, the secret to praying comes in positional maturity in the Christian's life, and a Christian will begin to become mature when, in his prayer life, he ceases to speak his needs and begins to live for others' needs and purposes. As we become more like Christ, we begin to live for others.

DADDY, DADDY

Now let's look at the real meaning of the Lord's Prayer, as given to us in the ninth verse. After telling them what should not be done, Jesus said, "After this manner, therefore, pray ye: Our Father which art in heaven, Hallowed be thy name" (Matthew 6:9 KJV).

Here we begin with that most important of all positions. That is the relationship of the Christian to God. Jesus opened the minds of the disciples to express to them the first statement that must be made, the salutation to God, "Our Father." There is so much in those two words that needs to be covered, but because of the length of this writing, we shall touch it only briefly. The disciples knew perfectly well what Christ was saying here, because of the way in which He approached it. The relationship of *Our Father* is the relationship of a daddy and His child. We are not to approach the throne of grace as mature adults, not even as adolescent children, or five to ten year olds, for at this period we have already begun to develop habit patterns and desires that will be retained for life. We are to approach God as very small children, two, three or four years of age, who at the sight of Daddy, are filled with great joy and anticipation. Our relationship to God should be as small children, anticipating the joyous presence of a loving father. As children of God we have been adopted into the family of God, and from that position in Ro-

mans 15, because of our deliverance from bondage
and fear, we should cry out, ''Abba, Father.'' In this
case, ''Daddy, Daddy.''

As a small child, when I first moved into the area
of North Houston, there was a well in our back yard
and before we put an electric pump over that well, in
order to get water, we had to use an old hand pump.
One dark night, I was asked to get some water from
the well. I was terrified of the darkness at that time
due to deep insecurities in my own life. My father,
sensing this, went with me. I remember there was no
fear with my father there with me—only joy. Therein
lies the position of this declaration as Jesus was teaching his disciples to say, ''Our Father.'' It simply
means that we should have such a longing for the
person that coming out of our hearts is that cry of
joyous longing in anticipation of God's promised
presence at the call of our voices. Our Father could
very simply mean, Daddy, I love you and I'm speaking to you. So again, Jesus says to His disciples to begin their prayers with excited anticipation as children
crying for their daddy. And, doing this will bring His
complete attention to you as you seek His presence
and protection in your life. How desperately important this posture is to any child of God going on in
the *Kingdom of God!* Without it there can be no answered prayer, for God is all-sovereign. He is our
Father, omniscient, omnipotent and omnipresent.

JEHOVAH

He then moved to the declaration of glory that
must always accompany praying in the life of every
Christian. His statement to His disciples was that
they must declare the glory of God as they prayed.

He said, "Hallowed be thy name." There is not room in this book even to begin to touch the true meaning of the name Jehovah-God. For instance, there is Jehovah Shamah, which means the Lord is present, always about us, always ready to meet our needs. There is Jehovah-Jireh, simply meaning God provides our needs—He will provide—it is a promise. Jehovah Repha means a promise of healing to our lives, not only physical, but spiritual. We have Jehovah-Nissa, meaning that God's banner is over us; He covers us with His banner; and Jehovah-Tsidkenu, God is our righteousness. The word righteousness means right standing with God. Then there is Jehovah-Shalom, meaning the Lord is our peace, our life, our shepherd, Jehovah is God. A good way to tell at what level you walk with christ and to what degree you live in the fulness of His person would be to see in your own heart what His name really means to you. Does just the concept or thought of God bring reverential awe to your heart—not in trembling at the terror of a circumstance, but being overwhelmed by just who He is? Joyously so.

You see, when Jesus was teaching His disciples how to pray, it was imperative that they look to God as the *father*, or *daddy* with longing, hope and desire for communion as well as communication. How desperately important it is for us to understand that prayer is finding the mind of God and agreeing with Him, and until we come to the place where our desires are overwhelmingly brought to a place of hope, we will never really know the fulness of Christ and the power that comes with that name! *Our Father which art in Heaven, hallowed be thy name* is the door into the mind of God. We must love Him more than we love ourselves. The central theme of our very beings must be caught up in His priceless Person. To enter into the realm of prayer, Jesus must be Lord, for prayer is not a position but a person, Jesus Christ!

THE KING IS COMING

As He goes further in the teaching, in the 10th verse, His statement to His disciples is, ''Thy kingdom come . . .'' Here Christ pulls back the curtain of the existence of every Christian who serves and desires to serve in the will of God. God has a perfect plan for every life. This is why there is so much in the Word of God that has to do with our not being rewarded for what we do for God, but for what God is able to do through us. It is from the posture of a servant that we receive our rewards. It is from the position of our being obedient that God is able in this kingdom in which we live to bring to pass His perfect will.

The *kingdom* is God's plan operating through our lives. Therefore, in order to get in on what God already has going, we must come to the place of being yielded to Him. In Ephesians 2:10, He teaches us that God, before the foundation of the world, laid out a path for every individual to walk. The person living, or walking, in that path or plan, will live the *good life.* It's already been prearranged and made ready for us, simply meaning that God has divinely put together a ministry for every individual. It is already written out in Heaven. So prayer puts us in the position of finding the mind of God and agreeing with it as we will share in a later chapter.

Again, as we stand before God someday, we are going to be given rewards based on our obedience.

Our obedience can come only if we present ourselves as not only living sacrifices holy, acceptable, as Romans 12:1 tells us, but as little children coming into the presence of Daddy and receiving instruction as to how to live that day. This is brought out in Matthew 16 and 18, in the area based on Christ's declaration of what is bound in Heaven will be bound on earth, and what is loosed in Heaven will be loosed on earth (Matthew 16:19 and 18:18). Therefore, as Christ was speaking with His disciples, He was saying to them that it was important to daily seek the Will of God for their lives, then to move into that will and let Christ operate His perfect plan through them.

"Thy kingdom come . . ." is God's plan for the life; ". . . Thy will be done . . ." is the agreement with that plan on earth; ". . . As it is in Heaven" is the declaration of that which is already done. We must be able to look into Heaven to see what is bound and loosed and then agree with it. That is living the life of prayer.

FRESH BREAD

He is teaching His disciples to look to the Father for their needs as He states, "Give us this day our daily bread." In this case, *children's bread* is that sustenance to the spiritual life as well as to the physical. Again, God will not give us stone for bread, but will meet the perfect need in the life of the individual who is yielded to Him, such as the widow who had little left, but when the prophet Elijah came, took what small amount of meal and oil she had and made a cake for him. He ate of her fare, and because her heart was in the grace of giving, she was never again to be able to empty that cruse of oil. God supernaturally kept it filled for the duration of the need. Herein is God that He meets both physical and spiritual needs of His children who look to Him in complete dependence. This volume could not contain the miracles performed even in my life pertaining to needs, that through prayer, God supernaturally filled. Not only did he fill the needs, but He brought declarations of praise and thanksgiving from my heart. How wonderful and loving is our great God who loved us so much that He sent the priceless person of Christ in the miracle of His virgin birth, to live His life without sin and to be taken because of our sins and nailed to a cross! Then as the answer to our sins, He was taken from that cross in death, only to live again—to come up out of the grave and be seated at the right hand of the Father. Oh Priceless Person, oh glorious praise, oh glorious thanks, Jesus' name is above every name! Thank you, Father! Our needs are met in His will, for by grace were we saved, and through that grace we have our living and our being, and by that grace, when it comes time to die, death will hold no fear or sting, but it will be a bridge to greater glory. This will bring us to His presence.

FORGIVENESS

We are faced with the position of forgiveness. Here Christ states, "And forgive us our debts as we forgive our debtors." We have already shared in the beginning of this book the basis of the forgiveness of sin. Money was an important measure in the life of the Jew. In fact, here Christ was dealing with the thing most important to the Jewish life (especially to the

Pharisee). The amount of a Jewish individual's wealth was a way to measure God's blessing to him. As in Job, it was thought a man of great wealth was a man greatly blessed of God. For a man to owe a debt to another and leave it unpaid was almost unforgiveable. Through Old Testament teachings we find that on a certain religious holiday, they came together to worship and settle their debts. Christ dealt with them at this level—that they were to forgive the debts and become forgiven of the debtors. May I share in the real meaning of the Lord's prayer, that if you have anything in your heart against another individual; if someone has ever harmed or hurt you and you have never forgiven him/her, then you should settle the issue at this moment, and I urge you to! Praise God for the hindrance, thank Him that it happened, and leave it behind, that you might truly enter into the realm of answered prayer—of not only hearing from God, but declaring in faith, believing what you hear. It is God's commandment that we do this.

We cannot have resentment in our hearts toward any person and have any prayer answered. God is emphatic regarding this. In order to achieve a prayer position with Christ, we must stand free of all resentment and unforgiveness.

Then He begins to close the teaching by declaration, as He urges the disciples to turn their lives completely over to God daily. Satan rules this world. He is forever trying to counter the Christian, by wiles, into a compromising position of his life. He wants to seduce him. He goes about as a roaring lion seeking whom he may devour, setting up circumstances, relationships, and conflicts, hoping that the Christian will succumb to his feelings, rather than to a position of praise in every negative experience. So in looking back into this prayer, we find that it is built in sequence.

A CHILD'S PRAYER

We find in the beginning—a child in the presence of God; longing for a relationship with the Father and desiring the will of God to come in his life. He is also standing in forgiveness, having forgiven those who have trespassed against him, and then crying out, "Oh God, I am incapable in my own flesh of coming against the wiles of the devil, so I thrust myself upon thee, saying, 'Father, lead me not into temptation, or bring us not into temptation. Keep a hedge about me that Satan cannot break through. God, bring me to the place that my eyes are upon thee, and that I shall walk in the light—that you shall be my path of righteousness; that for your name's sake I will constantly yield to your person. Oh God, I know my weakness; I know that I am tempted in all things, but a way has been made—a way of escape, and I speak His name—JESUS!' "

You see, as Christ was teaching, He was saying, "And lead us not into temptation. . . ," for He knew the origin of temptation was not the soul of man who was conceived in sin, but the origin of temptation was the tempter himself, Satan. He was sharing with His disciples that they must cry out to God to be separated and protected from the devil, his demons and their wiles. For, in the next phrase, it says, ". . . But deliver us from evil . . ." For the most part, this is a mis-translation—in fact, the original manuscripts add after evil the word, one. The *evil one* is Satan. The point is that we cannot, in our flesh, do business with the devil. He is a *god*, having power, and doing things in this end time even in the name of Jesus. He is attempting to make some think an experience is Jesus, and he's bringing some to worship feelings rather than the person, as pointed out in II Corinthians.

We must not encounter Satan on our own, but wrapped in the person of Jesus Christ. He is our shield, as well as our offense, as we come against the wiles of Satan. How crucial it is (as Christ said to the disciples) to have the presence of the person of Christ in order to be led out of temptation, and then (after Calvary) by His blood and the Word of faith, to be delivered from the *evil one*. At this point He was teaching His disciples to declare to God, "Oh God, deliver us from the temptation that is given to us by circumstances and by the wiles of Satan. We cannot fight it; we cannot even see him, for about us are persons without bodies. You must be our deliverance from Satan" (Ephesians 6:11). Here I have interjected again some principles from Ephesians 6 for the Christian after Calvary, for about us are demons, persons without bodies, whose one goal is to attack the human who is made in the image of God. It is only by the grace and person of Christ and His blood and the Word of faith that we can overcome the evil one. In fact, he has already been overcome, and we are overcomers if we truly understand the position of the Lord's Prayer and move into its power and its purpose.

Finally, we have the phrase, "For thine is the kingdom and the power and the glory forever. Amen." Now there is some question as to the validity of these words. Some earlier manuscripts have not included them. Regardless, to me they are simply a declaration of faith by spoken word, and I shall speak of them. In them we find the Christian coming to the place of praise. In the beginning lines he is brought to brokenness and to the awesomeness of God, declaring that he is wanting the will of God and the kingdom to be operational through his life. He is believing God daily for the bread, the sustenance, and the life, as well as the income which always comes to the child of obedience. He has come to the place where there is no hindrance in his life, no harboring of bitterness toward others who have spitefully used him. He has now sought God's plan and purpose for liberty and freedom from the move of Satan in his life. So because of that he has gone into what is known as *high praise*, as in Psalm 149. "For thine is the kingdom, and the power and the glory forever. Amen." What is being said here is, "Yes, thank you Father; praise Your name; You are my Lord, my master, my sovereign, my majesty. You are all in all; You are all that You want to be and I agree to that. Praise Your glorious, wonderful, precious name. Work out Your plan in my life; I agree with it; whatever Your desire is, do it." You see, the kingdom would be the will of God operational through your life. The power would be the energy, or energma, or the salvation plan working through your life as spoken of in Philippians 2:12-13. The glory then would be God receiving the praise of the life of the Christian attached to the vine bearing the fruit. For the fruit of a Christian is not another Christian; it is Christ producing His life through that individual. Christ was saying to His disciples that the real meaning of the Lord's Prayer is simply complete obedience to the will of God; the transformed life—that Jesus could extend His life through them. He was preparing them for life in abundance, not only in their day-by-day walk with Him, but on the day of Pentecost, yet to come, as they would be thrust out of the Upper Room, anointed in power, glory and victory, proclaiming a risen Saviour and a coming Lord. He was giving them living and life in overwhelming abundance, but also dying grace. Oh how beautiful to let the life of Christ live itself through us! For the real meaning of the Lord's Prayer is just to transfer our lives to His life, to let Jesus Christ be Lord. The next time you quote this familiar passage of Scripture that perhaps is the most memorized of all in the Bible, may you know its real meaning and its real life position! May you truly, as a little child, rush into the presence of your Father desiring, longing and seeking His presence, His glory and His life for your life! May you truly come to the posture of a person crying, "Daddy, Daddy, Daddy!"

CHAPTER FOUR

HOW TO FIND
THE MIND OF GOD

How many times have we been asked by concerned Christians the question, "How do I find the mind of God in a matter?" Searching the Scriptures for this most important doctrine, we have come up with several verses that have so much to do with prayer that we are making it an addition to this writing.

To begin with, we will use a verse that has meant so much to me in coming to the place of commitment based on the need within my life. An imperative is to approach any circumstance or need that we have as a part of God's plan for us. Therefore, we are to seek His wisdom and will in every matter. God's mind is given to us. It is up to us to come to the place where we can be sensitive enough to know and then to agree with the plan that He has. I think the greatest illustration of this is in Proverbs 16:3:

> *"Roll your works upon the Lord—commit and trust them wholly to Him; (He will cause your thoughts to become agreeable to His will, and so shall your plans be established and succeed."* (AMP)."

Although the book of Proverbs is thought to be, by scholars, the collection of sayings that were prevalent at the time of its writing and that Solomon had a great deal to do with the collection of these so-called colorful anecdotes, it is my personal belief that all Scripture is given by inspiration of God. Based on that, I believe the spiritual hand of God has been through the ages a constant guard over the truth that is to be presented to you and me in this day and time. Therefore, I feel it is possible to teach as doctrine the verse we have just shared with you from the Amplified Bible. Again, I believe it to be one of the greatest verses found in the Bible on bringing a person into position in answered prayer.

It begins with, "Roll your works upon the Lord." This is a declared statement of commitment, that the individual might be totally and completely yielded to Christ. And in the process he will transfer his life and mind so that Christ is able to bring His mind to that individual, thereby having His will exposed. I am reminded of how, to this day, burdens or loads are still carried upon the shoulders of those in the area of Israel and Jordan. Here, if a man were to take another man's burden, he could simply arch his back over the burden of the man bearing, put his arms in the loops, or holes, of those packs they carry, and as the other man pushed backwards, he in turn would gather the burden upon his own shoulders. In this I see the nature of this verse, as God commands us to roll our works upon Him.

Again, I am reminded of Romans 12:1-2, where we are to become ". . . Living sacrifices, holy acceptable . . . ," the Word declares, and that we are not to be *conformed to this world, but to be transformed by the renewing of our minds.* How desperately important it is for us to know that *our thoughts are not His, and our ways are not His.* When I pray, I cannot pray effectively without the revelation of God speaking of my mind, that I might come to that agreement to His will, as we will share later. Therefore, my works are to be His works; as I am to position myself in Christ, to gather His burden, revelation, personality and commitment. I am to be free of fleshly enterprises that have any kind of spiritual overtones. Perhaps another way to say it is that the most intimate relationship we have with God is our prayer life, and to come to a mature relationship with God is to yield that prayer life back to Him. In doing so, whether it be by revelation, or burden, or intercession, we might speak His nature, His words; we might agree with His plan, His purpose; we might operate at the level of His commitment. No individual will ever come to a place of power or service until he has entered into that relationship of fulness. God has a plan and a purpose for every life, as we have shared before. Again, even that most intimate relationship He has a plan for—our prayer life. Thus, He says, "Roll your works upon the Lord," or bring your life to Me and allow Me to bring through you My plan or purpose.

WHOLLY OR UNHOLY

He then states in that verse, "Commit and trust them wholly to me." In what are we to trust? We are trusting the ministry of our lives to Him. We are yielding ourselves—we are giving up completely to God, which is our reasonable service. We have transferred our selves, even as Colossians states in the third chapter, that Christ literally becomes our life. In praying, God listens to His own voice. He agrees with His own plans. Therefore, the mature Christian, the real prayer warrior, is the individual who moves into that experience of day-by-day crucifixion and dedication to the Person of Jesus Christ.

For again, God states that in rolling our works upon the Lord, we must commit everything to Him. We must trust Him. In fact, we must trust them *wholly* to Him, meaning simply that we are to commit ourselves fully to Christ, allowing Him divinely, through us, to work out His salvation plan. Ordinarily, Christians will relinquish time on a limited basis for a Sunday worship experience; some that are more dedicated will give a Wednesday night along with Sunday. Still others pray over their meals in remembrance to God. A smaller group will have a daily family altar where they enter into the Word of God to study to show themselves approved. Even fewer than that are dedicated to the position of praying several times during the day. However, in this verse, God is asking for total dedication. He is seeking the individual who will fully yield his life to Him that He in turn can, through that dedicated child of God, minister and thrust His will.

Our works are to be rolled upon the Lord. They are to be given fully and totally to Him. Our entire life experience is to be committed to the Lord Jesus Christ. Again, the word, commit, means to yield fully, and the word, trust, is not only to yield fully, but is to bring even the heart's action to commitment, to trust God with everything. The greatest ministries I've ever known have been those which have been operated in full commitment, where an individual was so committed to Christ, so totally in love with Him, that he would have given up everything for the cause of Christ. When he preached or served, God's hand and will were constantly in his life. His joy was in his relationship with Him; his peace was at the level of His filling with His Spirit daily in his life; he sought only a relationship with Christ. Subsequently, his ministry succeeded.

SAM CANNATA

There are always souls for the hire; there are always people to be preached to, or those to be ministered to. My thoughts at this juncture go to a doctor whose total life is committed to Christ. His companion and wife also lives at that level. When the Communists moved in to take over Ethiopia, Dr. Sam Cannata was incarcerated. The physical fate of this man seemed bleak. Those who knew him waited for a word of either his demise or release. Literally hundreds of thousands of people were praying for this dear man. Soon the word came—miraculously, he was turned loose. When he came home, his testimony was of the joy he experienced during his confinement, how God used his witness, and how the precious presence of Christ was always evident wherever he was. Basically, there was no fear, only victory in his circumstance. And yet, deep inside, his one thought was the burden for those whom he had left —those whom he had physically as well as spiritually ministered to in his mission post in Ethiopia. Today, at this writing, Sam Cannata, who has a unique ability as a great physician to garner about him the world's goods and physical blessings that come from the ministry of the healing arts to the physical body, is packing to move his wife to the Sudan; an uneasy area that could bring the same threat of death as be fore.

The greatest joy in life will come, as in this dear man's life, when as a Christian, you roll your works upon the Lord, and commit and trust them wholly to Him. It is from that point that life begins. However, let us return to the subject of prayer and take a step further. The person who has fully committed his life to Christ has a promise from God. For you who have longingly desired to find the mind of God in matters, His declaration is at this point, as the Scripture says—"He will cause your thoughts to become agreeable to His will." Again, the way to find the mind of God begins with commitment. It has its origin in yieldedness to the Spirit of God. For it is to the committed life that He causes the thoughts to become agreeable to His will.

The key word is *agree*. However, at this point, prayer in its origin begins with God. To be able to find out the mind of God, an individual must be able to hear from the Lord. God's promise is that if you are fully and completely yielded to Him, *He will cause your thoughts to become agreeable to His will*. God answers no prayers but His own. In fact, the Will of God is supremely important in prayer. To have the mind of God in order to operate in that agreement, one must be in a spiritual posture to have revelation brought to his or her mind. God will enter into the thought process of your life. One of my favorite sayings is, "When in doubt, don't." I know this to work, that when I walk in the Lord and have a doubt about a thing, to override that doubt is to put me out of the will of God. Not only that, but I cause conflict and enter into mistaken relationships. To find the mind of God and become agreeable with it is a process that comes only to the individual who can be yielded fully to the Lord. We repeat His promise —"He will cause your thoughts to become agreeable with His Will."

Again, God has a plan and a purpose in everything, and to move to that position of being able to agree with that plan and purpose, we must be totally sensitive to God's voice and will. To be sensitive is a position of obedience. Obedience is a servant's stature that brings the Master's mind into focus. How important this verse is to the dedicated Christian who wants to be effective in a time when there is such a desperate need for real prayer. God will establish your thoughts. He will bring His mind to your mind. He will bring His will to your will, so that you can confess it and agree with it, for He will cause your thoughts to become agreeable with His will. When that happens, here is the promise He gives in the rest of the verse: ". . . So shall your plans be established and succeed." Can you see the scope of this promise? True prayer is finding the mind of God and agreeing with it. It is being brought to a position of *will* so that His will shall be done in our lives as through our lives in agreement, for prayer is God's power through man.

Again, God promised us that our plans could be established and succeed. What are the plans? They are: the mind of God being brought to us; God's will being given to us in order that we might agree with it. It is established in our minds. Our thoughts are then correlated with His thoughts so that we can declare by faith that they are done, for faith is a position of action that comes when a person agrees with the Will of God in a matter.

How wonderful this declaration! For those who have sought for years to know how to find the mind of God, how simple it is, for God's mind is already given to the Christian who is totally committed and has yielded his life completely to Christ. In that relationship, He is able to minister through him according to His plan. You see, to the life that walks in fulness and complete sacrifice, it is promised that the thoughts he receives by intuitive revelation can be confessed as so. The reason is that he is literally agreeing with and doing the Will of God. There are those who are seeking direction for the future. They want to know God's will in a matter in their lives. What do they do? The same position is brought here —prayer is a relationship of the life to the Will of God. Again, it is not the position of the body. It is not just being on your knees or face with your head bowed. Prayer is a lifestyle—full commitment to Christ—walking in His Spirit and His will. For those who are looking for direction for their future, God says to those committed Christians who walk daily in complete obedience to the Lord Jesus Christ that their plans are established and therefore become successful.

JESUS NEVER FAILS

I have a friend whose favorite motto is, "Jesus never fails." The truth of that statement is beyond human comprehension; however, it can best be said that whatever God established, He finished. Our position is to find out the Will of God so that we can agree with the plan of God. In this He will establish in us what His plan is through us. Then we can receive from Him that which He desires to do, and choose to say, "Yes," with our lives. The carnal flesh wants to be a success, to succeed in everything. It needs recognition; therefore, it strives for its period of life to achieve and be recognized as successful. This comes by living to the fullest degree that the physical will allow and that the mental can absorb, and conducting directions into human experiences.

However, to succeed in the Christian life is to cease to be, to die to self, to give up to God. God made man for Himself; He gave him provision to have joy unspeakable, to have a life that flows. Answered prayer comes by revelation. It is given to us that we might know and find the mind of God and then agree. The writer of Proverbs tells us through God's inspiration, that if we will take our lives and commit them fully to the Lord, if we trust Him with all that we are, give up everything to him, that He will then bring to our minds His will. Then on the basis of His will coming to our minds, we will then agree. As we agree, at that instant our plans are established and we succeed. How desperate even at the moment are those who so need a word from God that they seek counsel from men with great hope inside that they are doing the Will of God! How tragic! God's will in the life becomes clear and more directive as that life finds itself more possessed of God's Spirit, simply because it desires to be one with Jesus Christ. Jesus never fails!

BEST LAID PLANS

God already has a plan worked out. It becomes alive in the person's life who is fully committed to

Him. We find this principle again in the book of Hosea, 14:2 (KJV):

> *"Take with you words, and turn to the Lord:*
> *say unto him, Take away all iniquity, and re-*
> *ceive us graciously; so will we render the calves*
> *of our lips."*

Here the Scripture commands us to take with us words and turn to the Lord. The first commandment is to turn to God and receive cleansing in our own hearts. For this is the requirement of prayer, to bring ourselves into that position of being able to hear from God. God will not speak to a corrupted vessel. God's ministry is only through those who operate in His Spirit and allow His person to minister to their lives. Again, the key is the word, agreeing, as we have already shared in this chapter and will again. own hearts. For this is the requirement of prayer, to bring ourselves into that position of being able to hear from God. God will not speak to a corrupted vessel. God's ministry is only through those who operate in His Spirit and allow His person to minister to their lives. Again, the key is the word, agreeing, as we have already shared in this chapter and will again. Confession is the foundation of prayer. Unless iniquity is taken away, we will not hear from God. One of the important provisions of this Scripture is that confession must be *stayed with* until cleansing comes by revelation, or better said, the release of *praying through*.

Years ago, I heard someone make a statement about *praying through*. At that point, I was not in such a spiritual realm that I could understand what he meant. Praying through bore connotations of things that to me were extra-Biblical experiences. However, as God began to minister to my own heart, in breaking, I realized that this phrase meant staying with God in a matter until the answer came, thereby giving us the assurance that it was done.

Now you must look very deeply at this Scripture to see what God is saying. You find that He is stating that we are to come to Him with words. The first thing we do is confess our sins. That means staying in that confession until finally victory comes within, for you see, the Bible says at this point, "Take away all iniquity and receive us graciously." Now what does receiving mean? It means to be brought to that place where we are accepted into God's plan and will for that matter. How desperately important it is for the Christian to understand that we are received at the level of our confession. In other words, we are to confess until that freedom comes within, because iniquity hidden and unconfessed in our hearts will always hinder the flow of God. Resentment in our hearts will always stop God's power to our lives. God will not speak to or through a dirty vessel, other than in conviction of its sin, and then only through chastisement and scourging as spoken of in Hebrews 12. The principle is to continue in confession and let nothing that is set up in our past experience stand in the way of God's flow through our lives. We are not to allow Satan to move in us, and to involve us in circumstances that bring bitterness to our hearts. For again, bitterness will stop revelation. Our confession and restitution must continue until we are brought free. Please understand that unconfessed sin and unresolved bitterness will always stop God's flow and power to the life.

Never try to become an intercessor or a possessor of God's purpose and plan until you are willing to meet God's flow and power to the life.

Never try to become an intercessor or a possessor of God's purpose and plan until you are willing to meet God's own formula for deliverance, for God sets the rules in the Word. To have power with God, the Christian must be right with Him. You see, you can never be used of God until the only thing that matters in your life is Christ. *Old things must pass away; all things then become new* . . . that nothing that has ever happened or has been done to you by man through Satanic dominion or oppression hinders God's flow to your life. You must stand in praise for the negative aspects of your person, thanking God for all that has transpired.

What happens at that point? Let's look at it again. He says, "Take with you words, and turn to the Lord, and say unto Him, Take away all iniquity and receive us graciously." Now upon iniquitous conditions being removed and our being graciously received, what happens? God moves into our lives and brings us His mind. We are then able to think with His mind; operate in His will, and pray the prayer that He desires to bring to pass. This is brought out in the rest of the verse where He says, ". . . So will we render the calves of our lips." What are the calves of our lips? It is God speaking through us. And this is because we are filled with His person. How desperately we need to know this doctrine that our prayer should be His prayer; our words, His words; our attitudes, His attitudes; our life, His life; our minds, His mind; as commanded in the Word of God. And what do we receive from that? For the first time, joy unspeakable, life in abundance, and again out of our innermost being shall flow that river of life that ministers to the needs of those without it. The greatest thing you can do for God is not to try to be *faithful in service*. It is not trying to tithe, or give, or make a sacrifice to serve in any capacity. The only thing that matters is for you to give your life completely over to Him, which, in fact, is your reasonable service. Then with that commitment comes all other things mentioned. You see, the greatest prayer warriors that history has ever known have been those who have laid aside their own lives and sought and received His life for theirs. The most intimate relationship that we have with God is our prayer life. Even this must be rendered unto Him. Wouldn't it be something, if the next time you pray, because you are broken over your own sins and brought into the right relationship with God, that you said, ''Oh, God, let me not pray until I pray Your words; let me not speak until I speak Your voice; I render, I give over to You the calves of my lips; give me Your will, Your intercession, Your position from the Word of God. I agree with it.''

COLD SNAP

Render is an unusual word. One of the things that usually brings rendering is heat. I am reminded of an incident of years ago. One of the real joyous experiences of my life was to be able to go home to any kind of family reunion. I'm from a little town in South Central Texas called Cuero. In my mother's family were eight children. In my childhood there were the joyous reunions of this family coming together, with its myriad of children. The times were

the late 30's. The summers would always be enjoya-
ble in that I would spend two weeks on the farm. At
that time, we were living in Houston, but during the
summer my family would send me back to stay with
an uncle who had a hundred acres, a wonderful wife,
and the finest of children. Those days would pass
quickly, and soon I would be riding the train back to
Houston, with hope reigning in my heart for another
trip back. This always came at the first cold snap. The
reason we looked forward to that freeze coming to
that part of the country was that we would again con-
verge upon this farm to do the things farmers knew
how to do—kill a hog! Again, these were joyous
times. I would not stay around for the killing, for
usually the hog they would kill for that winter would
have been an old friend that I had ridden that summer without permission. When it came to its demise,
I would hide. Later came all the things involved that
included the grinding and the stuffing of the sau-
sage, the cutting up of the meat, and hanging it up
in the smokehouse, with its wondrous odors, behind
the farmhouse. My aunt in those days did her washing in the back yard, in an old black washpot. However, on that day, there was no washing done in that
vessel; rather it was filled with the fatty remains of
that hog. At the day's end the fire was lit and soon
the contents were sizzling and finally boiling. Then,
while still warm, the grease was poured into large syr-
up cans. These were left to cool. Finally, with lids in
place, they were placed in the back of each car and
the grease then taken home and used in cooking.
How wonderful the memories of those earlier years!
The point is, the last process was always the boiling
down of the fat to make the grease—the rendering.

Rendering is changing something from one use to another—in this case, by fire.

I am reminded of Isaiah 6 where Isaiah saw God's glory, His light, and then he saw himself. He saw only light, for no man has seen the face of God and lived. When a man stands in the light of God with his own life and sees himself as he really is, he screams out from his own personal being how wretched and vile his life is. When Isaiah had that experience, God then proclaimed that He needed a man. And as always, when man is committed to Christ, he not only desires to be used, but anticipates the opportunity. There is a calling so strong within that he must submit to that position. But before Isaiah volunteered, something happened. God did a unique thing. He sent an angel with a live coal in his hand which had been taken off the altar with tongs. He came toward Isaiah with it and placed it upon his lips. He simply touched him and Isaiah's sin was purged. What brought that position? When Isaiah saw God, he saw himself, and when he saw himself, he screamed out, ''Woe is me, for I am undone, because I am a man of unclean lips and I dwell in the midst of a people of unclean lips; for mine eyes have seen the King, the Lord of Hosts.'' The point is that when man has confessed through the iniquity of his heart and has been received into the position of having placed upon him the Mind, Will and Purpose of God, in order to agree with it, that man operates in answered prayer. The coal was placed upon the lips of Isaiah, and when God said, ''Whom shall I send, and who will go for us?'' then Isaiah said, ''Send me.'' His lips had been purged; his heart desired one thing—to give his life to God, in complete fulness. Do you know what the fire of that coal did to the lips of Isaiah? It rendered them, just as the fire rendered that fat and changed it from one use to another. So shall the flame of God's purging be in our own hearts. Dear friend, answered prayer is finding the mind of God and agreeing with it. However, to have it, we must be broken; we must be purged; we must be absolutely and completely brought to that place where our desire is for Christ to consume us. How do we find the mind of God? Through the cleansing of our hearts and the rendering to God of our lips that He may speak through us. Again, the verse says, "Take with you words and turn to the Lord and say unto Him, 'Take away all iniquity and receive us graciously. So will we render the calves of our lips.' "

There is one final verse in this chapter that I believe would be appropriate to show us that we do not know what to pray for as we ought, and therefore we must render our lips to God to allow him to pray through us. Job 37:19 states:

> *"Teach us what we shall say unto Him, for we cannot order our speech by reason of darkness."*

The significance of the statement is I don't know what to pray for—I don't even know how to pray—other than God revealing to me His mind and His will.

This is what happened to Isaiah—he saw God, confessed, and then his heart was cleansed. Through this purging he became an instrument—a vessel, a servant of God. By the same token you and I are to do that to reach prayer power, revelation and the

mind of God. We must seek God's mind as to what
to believe Him for. This comes only through a broken, dedicated, consecrated, yielded life that is more
in love with Jesus than himself. It is this servant in
obedience whom God uses. From this position he
does not quote or chant prayers to God; but he simply lets God divinely relate to him His will and plan
and purpose. God has a plan for every Christian's
life. He knows what He wants to hear and do—it is
already bound and loosed in Heaven. He wants the
children of God to become so yielded to Him that
His mind becomes their minds, His ways their ways;
because, as obedient servants, they are led. The mind
of God is given to every Christian—the ability to receive it comes only in resurrected life or, said in another way, being filled daily with the Holy Spirit and
walking in His will.

Paul said it through inspiration in Romans 12:2:

*"And be ye not conformed to this world: but
be ye transformed by the renewing of your
mind, that ye may prove what is that good, and
acceptable, and perfect, will of God."*

Coupling that with Job, the statement is, "Teach us
what we shall say unto Him, for we cannot order our
speech by reason of darkness." With this in mind,
we can see that when Jesus taught His disciples to
pray, they were instructed in the area of yieldedness,
brokenness and openness to God's holiness in their
hearts. In doing so, they might in truth come to the
place where God's presence would be utilized in
their lives.

Learn to find the mind of God—it begins at the
position of being completely contrite, humble and

submitted (Isaiah 57:15) or, in other words, rendered.

CHAPTER FIVE

THE REAL MEANING
OF INTERCESSION

"So too the (Holy) Spirit comes to our aid and bears us up in our weakness; for we do not know what prayer to offer nor how to offer it worthily as we ought, but the Spirit Himself goes to meet our supplication and pleads in our behalf with unspeakable yearnings and groanings too deep for utterance.

And He Who searches the hearts of men knows what is in the mind of the (Holy) Spirit —what His intent is—because the Spirit intercedes and pleads (before God) in behalf of the saints according to and in harmony with God's will." Romans 8:26-27 (AMP).

In no other verses do we find a more specific declaration from God about our inability to know His mind. I am reminded of the Scripture that declares that our thoughts are not His thoughts; our ways are not His ways. In fact the only way His will can be discerned is to have Him cover our minds with His. The Scripture teaches that this should be done on our part. It is accomplished when we appropriate Romans 12:1-2, AMP.

> *"I appeal to you therefore, brethren, and beg of you in view of (all) the mercies of God, to make a decisive dedication of your bodies— presenting all your members and faculties—as a living sacrifice, holy (devoted, consecrated) and well pleasing to God, which is your reasonable (rational, intelligent) service and spiritual worship.*
>
> *Do not be conformed to this world—this age, fashioned after and adapted to its external, superficial customs. But be transformed (changed) by the (entire) renewal of your mind —by its new ideals and its new attitude—so that you may prove (for yourselves) what is the good and acceptable and perfect will of God, even the thing which is good and acceptable and perfect (in His sight for you)."*

Space would not allow the development of the deep meaning of these two verses; however, in summing up what God is saying, through Paul, to the church in Rome, we see that they must give of their total selves to Christ. They must be devotedly committed to His person. It is their reasonable service. Then He states that their minds must be renewed— an experience that comes when a person has crucified himself and walks resurrected in Jesus Christ. What a position! To think with the mind of Christ, to live by His thoughts, to act in His way, to pray His prayers— these come only in the transformed life.

Also, we find in Philippians 2:5 (KJV):

"Let this mind be in you, which was also in Christ Jesus."

Here is the command that we must have God's attitudes and purpose in life. We are to let His mind be ours.

Intercession is God's mind working through us to perform His purpose in another person or circumstance. In Romans 8:26 we find the evidence of this fact. To begin commenting on this verse, we must first establish with you that when you were saved the Holy Spirit came to dwell within you. At the moment of your new birth, God entered into your spirit with a daily plan for your life. His purpose is that through you He might continue His work here on earth. Consequently, the Spirit-filled (Ephesians 5:18) and controlled Christian walking in the Spirit (Galatians 5:25) will do the continuing work of Christ through his life. Again, you must understand that the Holy Spirit wants to consume you completely. He wants to move from within to cover you without, that He might be the *lamp unto your feet* and that He might be your attitude—your thoughts as you *dwell on things above.*

This intercession comes from above—those things already bound and loosed—those decisions eternal. The Scripture teaches that God is looking for *a man* (Isaiah 59:16). His eyes search to and fro for a person that is committed. What a privilege to be that person! What a blessing! What a ministry! Let's see how this kind of person operates.

As in verse 26 of Romans 8, "So too, the Holy Spirit comes to our aid and bears us up in our weakness. . . ." What aid and what weakness? Again, it must be understood that even though we are commanded to pray for those who have needs, we are also shown that it is God Who brings to us conviction as to what to pray for. As a rule of thumb, if you have a burden regarding a person or situation, you already have answered prayer. "For God is not the author of confusion . . ." (I Cor. 14:33) and He will never place upon an obedient Christian a false position. When you find yourself under a burden for another individual and you are walking with God, begin to praise Him, for He is using you in an intercessional position. Your prayer is answered. Shout the victory!

Remember, to operate in answered prayer you must know that the Holy Spirit comes to our aid and bears us up in our weakness. Our weakness, again, is that we do not know what to pray for or how to offer it worthily. God has His own plan for the Christian life. It includes His own plan for prayer. As we have shared before, God answers no prayers but His own. He listens only to His own purpose in prayer. The things that are to be done must originate from Heaven (Matthew 18:18). They are eternal things that have their bearing not only on the present, but on the future as well.

Therefore, our position is to yield to the Spirit's control and then let Him conduct His own business of prayer. His ways are the ways of God for He is God. He will approach God with our supplication in the right manner and plead in our behalf with unspeakable yearnings and groanings too deep for utterance. How beautiful! There are no words in the human language that can explain the depth of this phrase—God coming into the presence of God with His Will being given through an obedient vessel.

This is flow-through praying. This is real vine praying (John 15:7). This is true Christ-controlled praying—God speaking to God through the obedient Christian.

Incidentally, this kind of praying can be without utterance. That means the Christian who has experienced intercession can do so without words—no expressions orally to God, only deep flowings of His life through the Christian's.

He then explains what intercessory prayer really is by verse 27. His position here is that God knows all things of the present as well as of the future. It is His plan to overcome Satan, by exercising through prayer the defeat of the circumstances in the life of the person. God knows the needs of His kingdom and the saints that live in it; therefore, it is necessary (because we do not think with His mind) to come into *harmony with God's Will*.

Prayer is warfare, but it is God that chooses the time, place and weapons to be used. Prayer is the weapon. Intercessory prayer brings victory in every battle.

The key to all prayer is to find the mind of God and agree with it; to act in harmony with it; to let it flow through our lives; to let the Spirit intercede through us before God.

Obedience is the posture; intercession is the word; God is the Victor!

CHAPTER SIX

AGREEING WITH GOD

In this chapter, it is our intention to take you one step deeper into the position of praying. Before we can do that, there must be an explanation of the relationship that Jesus Christ had with the Father while He was here upon this earth. He was an extension of the Father upon this earth. His ministry was actually the ministry of God through Him. To understand that basic principle will bring you to the place where you can allow Christ to be Himself through you, for as Christ was with the Father, so are we to be with the Son. Jesus was an extension of the ministry of God. We are an extension of the ministry of Christ. His position was one of total obedience to the Father. In our position, we are to be totally obedient to the Son. His relationship was to let the world know that He and the Father were one. Our relationship is to be one with Christ, and as Christ, in his obedience, constantly agreed with what the Father desired to do, so it is with our lives that through us Christ might continue His ministry here upon this earth. The Bible says in I John 5:14-15 (AMP):

"And this is the confidence—the assurance, the [privilege of] boldness—which we have in Him: [we are sure] that if we ask anything (make any request) according to His will (in agreement with His own plan) He listens to and hears us.

And if (since) we [positively] know that He listens to us in whatever we ask, we also know [with settled and absolute knowledge] that we have [granted us as our present possessions] the requests made of Him."

Herein lies the secret to all praying; that is, finding the mind of God and agreeing with it. God commands us to do this, for the Spirit knows the need. Again, we are reminded of this in Romans 8:26, for through inspiration, God declares that we do not know what to pray for as we ought. In the chapter on warfare praying, we shared from Ephesians 6 that in order to literally do battle with the devil, we must pray in the Spirit. Jude 20 commands us to pray in the Spirit. Just as worship is in the Spirit and by the Spirit of God (so explained in Philippians 3:3), in the case of prayer, it is Spirit dealing with Spirit. From the level of human reasoning, we may see the need in another situation or circumstance of a person's life; however, we cannot deal effectively with it except on the spirit level. Herein is the promise given to us in I John 5:14-15. We are promised confidence, that assurance, that privilege of boldness which we have in Him. Why do we have the privilege of boldness? Because we can *come boldly into the holiest by the Blood of Jesus* (Hebrews 10:19). Again, we must understand the principle of Jesus as he ministered the

Will of the Father. He came as a beloved son into God's presence in order to do the Will of God and the purpose of God. This must be understood before you can see the truth of this chapter—that you and I are an extension of Christ, as Jesus was an extension of the Father. Therefore, as Christ came into the presence of the Father boldly, with confidence, as His Son, crying "Abba, Father," or saying "Our Father," and receiving in return a spiritual response from God, so must we.

Let's look at this privilege as expressed in the Word of God. Again, to understand that Jesus never worked a miracle is to understand our commission. Now before you cast this book down, let me share what I mean (Scripturally.) Then as it is revealed to you, you can choose to move to the dimension to which we are commanded in this scripture.

In John 5:17 (KJV) it says:

> *"But Jesus answered them, My Father worketh hitherto, and I work."*

To establish with you a base for this doctrine, you must understand Christ's meaning in ". . . My Father worketh hitherto and I work." The truth is that the ministry of Christ began with the Father. Again, He agreed with the Will of God, and God's plan and purpose were extended through His Son. By the same token, this is the position we are in. We are an extension of the Son. This in turn brings glory to the Father. Now with this position in mind, let me again say that the ministry of Christ began with the Father. He looked into Heaven, God expressed to Him what He was to do, He agreed with it, and allowed Himself to operate in it in the liberty of the Will of God.

Now you say, that verse doesn't say all of that. That is correct, but look at the 19th verse (AMP).

"So Jesus answered them by saying, I assure you, most solemnly I tell you, the Son is able to do nothing from Himself—of His own accord; but He is able to do only what He sees the Father doing. For whatever the Father does is what the Son does in the same way [in His turn]."

Here is Christ's answer to the Jews, who were seeking to kill Him for breaking the Sabbath, and for saying that God was His Father, thereby (making Himself equal with God). He looked at them and said, ". . . I assure you, most solemnly I tell you . . ." Now my question to you as a reader is, do you believe the Bible to be in error? Do you receive it as a literal proclamation, a declaration from the heart of God? Is there any question in your mind about its truth or validity? Then look at this verse, and if you can receive its truth, it will place you in a different dimension of living. Please understand that prayer is not the position of the body; it is a condition of the heart. Prayer life is the life which *exists in Christ daily* and through that life, Jesus Christ extends Himself.

JESUS NEVER WORKED A MIRACLE

In looking further into this position, let's continue with Christ's statement to those about Him. He said, ". . . I assure you, most solemnly I tell you, the Son is able to do nothing from Himself . . ." Now that was an unusual proclamation to these Jews. However, they were after Him for making Himself equal with God. Therefore, in explaining His ministry to them, His statement was that it was the Father Who was ministering life through Him—not Himself. Look at it this way. The blind saw, but only by the power of God and the obedience of Christ. The lame walked the same way. The maimed's hands were made whole. The leper's skin was made clean and without disease. Even the dead, at the voice of God through this man, came out of the grave, not only alive, but healed of their diseases. Christ opened His mouth to speak, but it was the Father speaking through Him. It should be the same way with us. Our conversation should be in Christ; the words we speak should come directly from Him. We should learn not to speak until spoken through.

His statement to those who were after His life was that He was able to do nothing for Himself, of His own accord, but He was able to do only what He saw the Father doing. Don't miss this. If your understanding is enlightened in this matter, it will get you out of the business of trying to live the Christian life, into the business of letting Christ live His life through you. Now in returning to His declaration, He said He could not do the miracles of His own accord, that it was the power of God. He was the son of God, but also the son of man. His one posture in this world was to be a sacrifice. He came to seek and to save that which was lost. Therefore, all the miracles that He performed in this world were simply flowers planted along His pathway to the cross. Therefore, His entire purpose for coming to earth was to die on Calvary, that He might seek to save that which was lost by the shedding of His blood, that by the Word of faith and the blood of Christ we know salvation and deliverance.

So His earthly supernatural ministry was actually

the Father doing it through Him. Christ walked in such a relationship with the Father that God was His mind. We are commanded to let Christ be ours. Again, we find in Philippians 2:5 and Romans 12:1-2, that we are to receive revelation and direction, and then to be in such a posture with Christ, that even the words we speak will be His words. For you see, Jesus is at the right hand of the Father, not only making intercession for us as our advocate, but at the same time committing His ministry and life through us.

In continuing the verse, we find ". . . For whatever the Father does is what the Son does in the same way in His turn." In the light of this statement we are reminded of the scriptures found in Matthew 16:19 and 18:18, that we are to live in such a way that whatsoever is bound and loosed in Heaven shall be revealed to us and that we can agree with it. In doing so, we allow the Spirit of God to move in us in that manner. Christ always chose the Will of the Father. Would to God our position would be the same way; that we would love Christ more than our own lives; that through us He could continue His will and way!

I CAN OF MINE OWN SELF DO NOTHING

As we continue with this thought, let's look at John 5:30 (KJV).

"I can of mine own self do nothing: as I hear, I judge: and my judgment is just; because I seek not mine own will, but the will of the Father which hath sent me."

Here, Christ again makes the statement, "I can of mine own self do nothing. . . . " During His earthly ministry, Christ was an extension of His Father, in that whatever God was doing, He was doing also. Such is the essence of prayer, the Will of the Father being presented through man, in the Name of His Son, Jesus Christ. In prayer we must follow Christ's example of total obedience to the Father and agree with Him by faith. Then we can pray the prayer of "binding and loosing" (Matthew 16:18-19). We must realize that we can do nothing from ourselves in the flesh. It must be Christ extended through us. This must be the desire of our heart. The only sign of maturity in the Christian is answered prayer, nothing else. In every case, when Christ was confronted by Satan or his demonic strongholds, He, through prayer, brought the Will of the Father into every matter. It is by God's Power that the enemy is overcome. By the same token, it is imperative that we bring, into every situation, God's Will. Then we can, through Christ and His Blood, destroy the works of the devil (I John 3:8). Our adversary fights to hinder or destroy the Christian's prayer life, for by prayer are he and all his principalities bound and stripped of all power. The Christian who attempts to live the Christian life by law and prays for his own will to be done, will always be powerless, confused, and overcome by the destroyer (Revelation 9:11). On the other hand, the Christian who is one with Christ will bring His life to their needs and strongholds, by entreaty; for out of their innermost being will flow that "river of living water" (Christ's life and will). This is the ministry of Jesus Christ through us. Prayer is not the position of the body, but the condition of the heart, being able to intuitively hear from God (Hebrews 5:14) concerning His Will and then, by faith, believing Him for "substance" (Hebrews 11:1). Always remember, as Jesus was with the Father, so are we to be with the Son — One (John 17:23).

The essential truth, then, of John 5:30 is that Christ sought only the Father's Will and acted upon it, believing. Therein, the blind saw, the crippled walked, the possessed were freed, and the dead came out of the grave; PRAYER!

Now, as we continue in this verse, we see that Christ declares His position, " . . . as I hear, I judge: and my judgment is just; because I seek not mine own will. . . . " Again, the imperative of prayer is the Will of the Father. Christ always chose the Will of the Father instead of relying on His own will. The result was that His decisions in every matter were always the Will of God. How paramount are these truths that must be realized by every Child of God that desperately desires to go on with God. The ministry of Christ was the Father acting through Him. We read this in many Scriptures in the Book of John (6:38, 7:16, 8:18, 26, 42, etc.). Christ sought not His own mind nor His own will, but only the Will of the Father, as He was constantly in prayer. When praying, He did not trust in His own perception or sense of what was needed. Not one time in His three years of God's ministry through Him did He change any situation, without first finding out His part in the Will of God through prayer. Jesus was so committed to the Father and yielded to Him that He had no desire to benefit Himself or to even have any aims or purposes of His own. His desire was to only do the Will and pleasure of the Father. I would to God that we would have such a desperate, dedicated love for the Lord that it would bring us to such a place where we could be trusted with His Will (Romans 8:26-27), committed to His Way (Romans

12:1-2), and that the world, encountering our lives, might turn its face to Christ and cry out, "I believe, I believe, I yield." This is my prayer for every reader of this book. As Jesus was One with the Father, so it might be in us — "Christ in you, the hope of glory"; RESURRECTED LIFE.

Again, this can only be when we have reached the place of having transferred ownership of our lives; that includes even our most intimate relationship—our prayer life—back to the Lord Jesus.

In the light of this, let's look at real praying once more. Looking back at I John 5:14, we read, "Now this is the—confidence, the assurance, the (privilege of) boldness—which we have in Him. . . ." Notice that capital "H" in Him—it is Christ. We are promised this truth, " . . . That if we ask anything (make any request) according to His will (in agreement with His own plan) . . . " we shall receive our request. Now the key to prayer, again, is to find the mind of God and agree with it. God has a plan, a definite purpose for every life. He has a direction for every individual. We receive it by revelation and discernment. In Ephesians, Paul said in chapter 1:17-18 (AMP):

"(For I always pray) the God of our Lord Jesus Christ, the Father of Glory, that He may grant you a spirit of wisdom and revelation—of insight into mysteries and secrets—in the (deep and intimate) knowledge of Him,

By having the eyes of your heart flooded with light, so that you can know and understand the hope to which He has called you and how rich is His glorious inheritance in the saints—His set-apart ones."

Paul's desire for the church at Ephesus was that

they might know what fullness, revelation and declared glory were in their lives. In another area of Scriptures (Colossians 1:27), we find this said in another way, " . . . Christ in you, the hope of glory." This is stated to another church, in another setting, but it is the same position. What a joy it would be for us to learn that agreeing with God is revelation praying, to take the most intimate relationship we have and give it back to God, thereby recognizing that He has a daily plan and purpose for our lives, and that we must submit to it; that we must give up to it, in order to serve. We must let His will operate in our lives; this is obedience.

Once more, praying is receiving the Will of God and agreeing with it. As Jesus was with the Father, in agreement with His plan, so are we to be with the Son, for God has a plan for our lives. Prayer is an act of obedience, for He states that our requests should be according to His will, and in agreement with His own plan. Another way to say it is, "God answers no prayers but His own. He listens to no prayers but His own." He has a plan. So answered prayer is finding out what has been bound and loosed in Heaven and declaring it by faith as if it were already done. Who has the right to do this? James 5:16 says:

> *"Confess to one another therefore your faults— your slips, your false steps, your offenses, your sins; and pray (also) for one another, that you may be healed and restored—to a spiritual tone of mind and heart. The earnest (heartfelt, continued) prayer of a righteous man makes tremendous power available—dynamic in its working."*

In the latter part of James 5:16, we find that the

prayers of righteous men avail much. What does the word, righteous, mean? It means right standing with God—one who has placed God in complete control of his life. This person operating in righteousness can literally have the greatest influence of any human at this period of history. Answered prayer begins in Heaven and is a living relationship of one who operates in obedience here on earth. God wants us to agree with His plan and purpose. He wants us to be able to hear what the need is; He wants to be able to capture the heart or knosis of the individual who is so committed to Him that He can transfer His prayer to them by epiknosis or intuitive revelation of purpose, that it be agreed with and answered. How many men, blind physically or spiritually, are waiting today for one individual who is committed to Christ? How many lame? How many maimed? How many spiritually dead? Through whom will God bring the next revival in history? What are His plans for these final days that include the changing of men's natures, for the glory of Christ and the church? What is He really wanting to do for the nations of the world that are waiting for one concerned individual, broken and yielded to the Spirit of God? One so committed that upon awaking each morning, he turns his heart to Christ and says, "Father, I agree with what is written in Heaven for my life today," and then lives it.

AMEN, SO BE IT

Now let's look at I John 5:15 where a promise is given when God says,

"And if, since we (positively) know that He listens to us in whatever we ask, we also know (with settled and absolute knowledge) that we

> *have (granted us as our present possessions) the requests made of Him.''*

There are two important things here that must be seen.

First, God listens only to His own prayers, for God's promise is that what we ask is given to us if we ask it in His will.

Secondly, we can know, with settled knowledge in our hearts, that if we do ask in His will, believing, it is already done. The Bible says that we have granted to us as our *present possession* the request made of Him. Now think of this for a moment. God has a plan. It is being worked out in our obedience. Our hearts are committed to Him. We are yielded fully to His will. Our lives (as well as our prayer lives) are given over to Him completely. Our greatest desire is oneness with the Lord Jesus. We want to walk in the Spirit, be filled with the Spirit, led of the Spirit, have the mind of the Spirit and pray in the Spirit. God sees that relationship so He places upon us a burden (with or without our knowledge of what the burden is). In an intercessory position we receive a burden that only comes as groanings which cannot be uttered. We have been given such a responsibility of prayer, that God will not even share with us what it's about. We just bear the heaviness and the load. However, in praying it through, there is suddenly a release, a great victory, and a great peace. We know it was done, and though we may not have known what was done, God used us to intercede for another individual's circumstances. In this case it is not our right to know, but only to be obedient.

THE FINAL STEP

Now, when does a person who operates in obedience have answered prayer? Before he prays. God says that when we agree with His will and pray in that agreement, we are granted as our present possession the request that we have made. Present means it's already ours—it's already there. Like salvation, it's already been paid for, already been done; we are just to receive it as a finished work. We are broken over our lives; we desire salvation through the confession of our sins. Then, through real repentance, we are brought into New Testament New Birth—born again—completed. However, the work was done 2,000 years ago at Calvary. Now when we pray in the Spirit we have the promise that we have already received as our present possession the request made. How wonderful! To look into Heaven and see what is bound and loosed; to say, "Yes, I agree"; to live in such a position first of all to receive revelation, and secondly, to live in such a faith position that we can agree with that revelation—how wonderful! Herein is the instrument wherewith God brings His grace and glory to the nations. We are commanded to pray without ceasing; we are commanded to pray for those in authority; but most of all, we are commanded to pray. Prayer brings you to that position of God's flow through your life.

This is again established in Jude 20 where He states:

"But you beloved, build yourselves up (founded) on your most holy faith, make progress, rise like an edifice—higher and higher—praying in the Holy Spirit."

(AMP)

We must find the mind of God. We must operate in

it. For the world has yet to see what one individual, agreeing with God, living in hope, can do simply by faith praying. I urge you to be that one. Every revival in history can always be traced back to one individual so committed to God that through agony of soul, Satan was defeated and revival came. As God searches for the man, will His eyes stop on you? They will if you love Him with all your heart and live only for Him. I trust that you will cry out now from your life, ''Oh God, here I am, send me!''